Creating Utopia
Living Life as a Miracle Worker

Workbook

Suzy Bootz

Although the author and the publisher have made every effort to ensure the accuracy and completeness of information contained in this book, we assume no responsibility for errors, inaccuracies, omissions, or any inconsistencies contained herein. Any slights of people, places, or organizations and unintentional.

First Printing 2016

ISBN 978-0-692-70434-9

ATTENTION CORPORATIONS, UNIVERSITIES, COLLEGES, AND PROFESSIONAL ORGANIZATIONS: Quantity discounts are available on bulk purchases of this book for educational, gift purposes, or as premiums for increasing magazine subscriptions or renewals. Special book or book excerpts can also be created to fit specific needs. For information, please contact suzy@suzybootz.com

Contents

"When one soul awakens to the reality of its own perfection, a light is magnified that lights up another's soul awakening. The tide of love is beyond measure. For you and I are one, and I am one with every soul you encounter. Thus in your awakening your energy awakens another from their illusion."

Excerpt from Through the Eyes of Truth:
A Conversation with God about My Life, Your Life, and Discovering our Purpose

INTRODUCTION

What would you do if you heard the voice of God speak to you? Would you recognize the voice of Source or would you disregard it as the voice of your own imagination? As someone who believes in God and the power of prayer, I heard God whisper into my soul a very specific message. "I want you to document your dream journey, so others will be inspired by your truth and realized they are never alone. I hear their thoughts, I know their voice, and I feel their cries." What if God spoke those words into your soul and asked you to write your journey so others could be inspired by the power of prayer? What would you do? How would you respond? Would you answer the call?

This question seems so simple yet God whispers into *your* soul everyday so how did you respond? What would you say when God asks you to believe in a dream so great that the world around you would consider it luck? If God says to you, "I want you to trust me. Trust me to the extent that you believe in the power of your dreams before they are even realized. Do you have the faith to do this?" How will you respond when you hear the voice of truth resonating within the walls of your soul, asking you to step up and own your faith? What if God asked you to believe in the message you were receiving to the extent that you had to write your prayer journal out word for word? Only then the world would look back at your journey and realize they must look within to hear the voice of their own truth.

Every day we are called upon to trust the voice of God yet we doubt that voice which we hear is actually Source energy. We are more willing to believe that others heard us reaching out to them through an email or a telephone call, yet are less willing to believe that God, our own Source of life, heard our call. Why? At what point in our life did we learn to disregard the voice of truth for the voice of fear? When were we so willing to acknowledge our own fear and illusion and convince ourselves of something that isn't real? As children of God we are born into the truth that our connection with our Creator is the most important relationship we can have. Yet as we grow into adults we learn to adopt the voices of fear in order to be accepted by the world around us who is worshiping illusion.

What if God has been speaking truth into your soul for years and rather than disregard the message, you listened. Really listened to the answers to your prayers. What would your life be like if you learned to silence the noise from the world outside of you, and tune into the sound of Gods voice resonating through the walls of your soul? I learned to tap into the voice of God and wrote my first book in the Through the Eyes of Truth series, titled ***Through the Eyes of Truth – A Conversation with God about my Life, Your Life, and Discovering our Purpose***. The words were literally the answer to my prayer when I asked God to show me my truth and help me to discover my purpose.

What happened from that moment on was that God showed me my truth by revealing to me my passion and my purpose. I learned that my passion was writing, just as it had been since I was in the third grade. I felt very connected to something greater than myself when I would put pen to paper. I discovered my purpose when God revealed to me through my passion of writing, that my purpose was to connect you to God by reminding you that we are never alone. God loves us more than we can ever imagine, and we never actually die but pass on from the physical to the energetic level. You could say that I discovered my purpose through my love for writing.

Have you ever asked yourself what your purpose is in life? Better yet, when was the last time you asked God a question and waited long enough to hear the answer? If you knew that every prayer you prayed was felt, heard and acknowledged, would you pray more and listen longer? This takes not only shifting your attention within, but getting comfortable in your own soul and establishing a relationship with God. This relationship also takes the faith to believe in your calling and the courage to walk the path alone. Are you ready to do this? I asked myself this question before I began every book I have ever written... and especially this book.

God spoke into my heart several years ago that I would be documenting my dream journey so others would not only believe in the power of prayer, but once again believe in the power of God. This dream journey began when I lost my mother in 2004 and I had to understand on a soul level the truth that we are all connected. Once we pass on from our physical body, our souls are still very much alive. Even though we can no longer see or be with our loved ones once they pass away, we are still very much loved by them, comforted by them, and reminded by them that this life is just an illusion.

The reality lies within the walls of our soul where we are connected to Source energy through the oneness that is life. We have never been apart from God except through our illusion of being separate from Source. Once we change our perception and realize the power of our dreams are within us, then we realize the connection we have to the miracle of life. My miracle of life encourages me to write and live out my purpose with a grateful heart and an open mind.

These pages were my introduction to Creating Utopia, a place where all is perfect and where miracles happen. Now I am going to leave the rest of these pages to be filled with my answered prayer. You see, in my quest to enjoy my love for writing I learned that God connects to me when I connect to God. So when I continually heard God whisper into my soul to begin my dream journal I knew it was time. Creating Utopia is about creating love and connecting to a place within me where the experience of love, joy, and peace is created. All I have to do is just connect to my "utopia" within my soul instead of looking for it in the world outside of me. Inside of all of us lies something that is our own soul imprint. We can't learn it from the world outside of us but instead remember it from the world within us.

Utopia represents life, love, and endless opportunities. For me it represents a place to call home, but not necessarily the home which is built from bricks and mortar. Rather the home that resides within our souls where every dream is a possibility and where we are all one with God. Where we are all one with each other through the power of God whether we are in the physical or spiritual realm. This is my story and it will be filled with the pages of my life that are deliberately created to share with you how dreams are created through the power of prayer and faith. Utopia is love. Utopia is life everlasting. Utopia is oneness where we are all experiencing ourselves as a part of the greater whole. This is only my perception of how dreams are created when God whispers into our soul and asks us to answer the call. I believe that God speaks to us throughout our moments yet we are so consumed with the world around us that we fail to hear His voice.

Sometimes miracles need to be created in order to awaken us out of our trance and remind us that we can write the story of our own lives through the hand of God. Each of us have the power to create miracles in our lives. We only need to remember that we are not defined by our circumstances, rather by our Creator. Abundance is not for the special or lucky...abundance is our birthright. So I ask you again, what would you do if God whispered into your soul and asked you to answer the call? Your journey is only one prayer away.

Last night I had a dream. Before I went to bed I prayed and asked God that I be shown how to achieve my greatest vision for my life. In my dream I was driving down a road that ended up in a dead end. I heard God speak to me and tell me if I wanted to push beyond my daily repetitions of fear, I was to turn the car around and literally drive in the opposite direction of where I was heading. Just before I woke up, I remember smiling and thinking to myself, "this is what it feels like to be on track to the greatest vision of my dream." Then I awoke and knew what I had to do. I had to create a miracle in my own life.

Together, let us reach for a dream so great that someone would label it as a miracle if you achieved it. Why not? What I have realized is that as children of God we have the power to create the life of our dreams. Yet as creatures of habit we create our lives through patterns of thoughts, emotions, and actions. My goal is to walk you through a journey that will push you beyond your conditional expectations and rise above any self-imposed limitations you may have established in your life. Whether your dream is to win a fitness competition, a car or a new house, the process is still the same.

Competition is only a perception of an illusion. You are not competing with another from a position of lack, but instead you are tapping into your greatest potential and connecting to God within to create that very experience you are trying to "win." You will realize in any perceived contest; you are **not** competing but *creating*. You are creating joy and a state of bliss for your life... you are creating *utopia*.

Creating Utopia
Living as a Miracle Worker

UTOPIA – A STATE OF BEING WHERE ONE EXPERIENCES BLISS AND PERFECTION

When you look in the mirror, what do you see? Do you see the eyes of a miracle worker staring back at you? If not, then maybe now is the time to shift your perspective and realize the gift that you really are! Every day I work with clients as a personal development and spiritual coach, and realize that so many of us don't truly know who we are. With the advances of technology, it appears that the social media has taken over our life to the point where you may be spending more time witnessing another person's experiences rather than creating your own. How have you lost the connection with yourself to the point where you would rather watch the experiences of a stranger than create your own miracles from within?

What if I could take you on a journey into self-discovery? Would it be worth putting the phone down and focusing on yourself? What if during this journey, you gained knowledge about yourself and could release self-imposed limits. Possibly limits that have been created by illusions of who you think you are rather than who you really are? Every day you witness people win contests and experience abundance of joy and passion. However, what if these experiences were in fact creation rather than based events based on luck? You have goals and miracles within you just waiting to be created, but how can you experience these miracles if you are focused on the world outside of you?

Creating utopia is about aligning with your greatest goals… whatever they may be. Since utopia is a sense of experiencing bliss and joy, then you could learn how to develop a relationship with yourself to a level you may have never experienced before. Furthermore, in this journey into self-love you created self-acceptance and self-sufficiency. While you are on this miraculous journey into self-discovery, you also have the opportunity to develop a deeper relationship with God. A relationship where you get to experience the intimate moments of connection through conversation. What a blessing. Then take this miraculous journey one step further where you may get to discover what your greatest goals are. Those experiences that bring your heart and soul the greatest joy, to the point where you no longer feel the need to live vicariously through another person's journey on the social media.

How do you do this? First you stop looking at the world outside of you for answers to discovering your purpose, and you seek those answers from within you. My journey began with a prayer and this is where I suggest you begin yours. Prayer opened my eyes and my heart to a deeper relationship with God, and myself, which eventually led to connecting to my goals and finding my purpose. To help you discover your own. God took me on an amazing journey where he shifted my focus from a world of fear to a world of love and possibilities. This journey required that I walk in faith and seek only his guidance when it came to understanding what I was capable of. Interestingly enough, God took me on a journey into the world of perceived competition. However, what if you could peek into the world of perceived competition and see it for what it really is…a creation.

With every step of faith, I learned to hear Gods voice so clear that I could recognize it when God spoke to me. Whether these words were whispers into my soul, or clear messages in dreams, I learned to separate truth from illusion. Looking back now, I understand the greatest lessons I discovered about creation. We are all creators and don't need to see the world from the eyes of fear. Everything you wish to experience begins within you, and when you choose to focus your thoughts, emotions, and actions on those experiences you wish to have in your life, then aligning with them creates the manifestation of them. A goal is your soul's self-expression of creating love and joy within you. There does not need to be an audience for you to enjoy the music of your own soul's creation. Maybe it was created so God could know himself through your creation. Isn't God audience enough?

I designed this workbook to correspond with my book, **Creating Utopia – Living Life as a Miracle Worker**. This book was just one of my answered prayers where I learned how to develop a relationship with my goals and deepen my relationship with God in the journey. My first book, *Through the Eyes of Truth – A Conversation with God About My Life, Your Life, & Discovering Our Purpose* revealed to me how to have a deep connection with God and to learn to love myself through his eyes. It empowered me and allowed me to release the need for approval from the world around me, and focus on creating those experiences my soul loved.

Let's create the journey together and everyday discover something new about yourself in the process of achieving your goals. I am going to take this journey with you and create my own personal goal in the process. Today is a great day to begin creating utopia… a state of being where we experience bliss and perfection. So here it goes… Creating Utopia Day 1…

"What some consider luck as they witness the manifestation of another's dream is seldom understood for truth. Which is the love and passion this soul used to create that which the world seeks to label as luck. If you dismiss the creation of abundance with another's luck, then you disregard the absolute truth that you can create what your heart truly desires through self-love, self-acceptance, and self-sufficiency. My child, you have witnessed this truth in the world around you, and have seen many fall from their own grace. You are about to unfold a truth so deep, that this dream journey will be written in order for all who seek the truth of their own existence to understand. They will not doubt that they too have the power to turn thought into abundance of that which brings them joy."

Excerpt from Through the Eyes of Truth
A Conversation with God about My Life, Your Life, and Discovering Our Purpose

Creating Utopia
Living as a Miracle Worker Day 1

LISTEN TO YOUR HEART

Although this may appear to be a simple request, I think most of us realize how difficult it can be to tune out the noise from the world outside of ourselves and tune into our own God whisper. Whether you are on a journey to discover yourself through entering a fitness competition or challenging yourself to be a better version of who you were the day before, we need to listen to our internal GPS. How many times in your life have you heeded the advice of another person only to regret your decision, because you knew in your heart that wasn't the right decision for you?

In order to be a miracle worker in your own life, you must trust your own voice and honor it. Take quiet time to know how you communicate with yourself and most importantly, how Source communicates with you. When you meditate or take alone time, you must sit in silence and not only listen for answers to your prayers but understand the difference between your own muffled thoughts created from fear from those powerful messages derived from love. The journey through any competition allows us the chance to reconnect with ourselves on a deeper level.

If we are connected to Source and co-creating our lives and our journey with God, then wouldn't it make it more meaningful to have the source of our greatest goals as part of the co-creative process? We learn through competition that in order to see beyond the physical senses we must see through the eyes of truth. The crown is not the end goal but instead the chance for our soul to experience something that connects us to a greater meaning ultimately becomes the sought after prize.

When I help my clients understand how to create a goal through perceived competition, the first thing I help them understand is that their ultimate goal already exists within them. Their role in the journey is to connect with their heart and listen for the God whisper to help guide them along the way. Only then will you be able to realize you were never separate from the love you wanted to experience as a creative being. I believe that the ultimate goal is to understand and accept yourself on a deeper level which is a greater gift than any crown, banner, or prize will ever provide you.

Trust your instinct and reach beyond what you have previously accomplished so you can experience a greater version of yourself. Know the limitations you imposed on your greatest dreams have been set in place by you so they can be removed by you as well. Understanding what fear created those limitations will help you perceive a new reality. As a personal development and spiritual coach for 8 years I work with women of all ages on a daily basis and realize the majority of our self-imposed limitations are created from feeling unworthy.

If you fail to acknowledge your own worth then it becomes increasingly difficult to convince yourself that you deserve to live out your greatest dreams. I believe the strongest emotions will always win, so if your fear of not feeling worthy is greater than your love for creating joy through an accomplished goal, then the stronger emotion of fear will win. It doesn't matter how much time you put into your training, you will always do something to sabotage your progress. Dig deeper into your own soul and grow beyond your own comfort zone. Then you will look at your life and realize you live in a world of possibilities where you can create your own miracles. Have fun and live your life as the Miracle Worker you are!

What is my "Utopia?"

_____

_____

_____

_____

_____

_____

_____

_____

How will experiencing this change my life?

_____

_____

_____

_____

_____

_____

_____

_____

What are my self-imposed limitations and what is my truth when it comes to these illusions I have created from fear??

_____

_____

_____

_____

_____

_____

_____

_____

_____

_____

_____

_____

_____

_____

_____

_____

"Whatever your heart and soul seeks in love, ask God and it shall be given unto you. For you are all extensions of Source energy, and cannot be separate from love except for your perception of the separateness. Seek that which your soul wishes to experience in love, and you will witness your world flow abundantly in love."

Excerpt from *Through the Eyes of Truth*
A Conversation with God about My Life, Your Life, and Discovering Our Purpose

Creating Utopia
Living as a Miracle Worker Day 2

CREATING A NEW NORMAL

So many of us are creatures of habit and we create our lives through patterns of repetition. Whether we are on a journey through self-improvement or on a journey through reaching life goals, we ultimately repeat the same patterns of creation. Our thoughts remain the same which subsequently create the same familiar emotions of love or fear, which lead us to act in accordance to those thoughts and feelings. However, what we often fail to realize is the truth that we create much of our life experiences from our patterns. If you don't believe me, then write out what you did from the start of your day Monday to this point in your day today. Patterns, patterns, patterns.

How is it that we create the same patterns and expect those same habits to create different experiences? In order to create new experiences of competing, having more joy in your life, or creating a goal from your inner kingdom, you need to create new patterns that will support the creation of the ultimate goal. However new patterns are not comfortable for us, because we often create our comfort level through repetition. That is one of the reasons advertising works so well. A new product is introduced into our environment and through repetition of their name and services, we grow comfortable with them and then become their customers.

Life goals are similar to the extent that you need to become comfortable with a new "normal." Ask any of my clients and they will tell you my motto in life is to "get you comfortable being uncomfortable." I have to get you to a new comfort level so you create new experiences. So often we are not taught what it feels like to achieve a goal that would have once been unimaginable to you. Because of this you have no frame of reference except for your imagination, faith and your co-creative power. All three are amazing ingredients to creating the life of your dreams!

Use your thoughts to paint a new picture of a specific goal you wish to experience. As you are vividly creating this goal, I would like you to allow yourself permission to feel the emotions of already experiencing this goal. What does it feel like? How is your life different today knowing you already have it? Then I ask you to begin acting today as if it is in your reality and support your thoughts, emotions, and actions already having this dream.

Whether you are attempting to experience winning a contest, a life goal, or creating a new home, the goals are different but the process is the same. Remember that Utopia represents a state of mind where you are already experiencing your greatest joy, your spiritual bliss, and the perfection of who you are. You don't need to seek this outside of yourself, since you already have the power to create these things from your own God given creative energy. We are all children of God and abundance of everything that brings us love and joy is our birthright. Stop telling yourself that you are not worthy of having the life of your dreams.

Since Source is experiencing life through you, don't you think you deserve to bring yourself the greatest amount of joy throughout your life? You are not defined by your experiences or another person's perception of you. The only eyes you need to see yourself through are the eyes of truth... the eyes of God. Be present in your moments throughout your life and be deliberate in creating new experiences so you can continue to push beyond your comfort level and grow in all areas of your life. Have fun and live your life as the Miracle Worker you are!

What patterns have I created in my life that no longer serve my higher good?"

_____

_____

_____

_____

_____

_____

_____

What fear based emotions have I grown comfortable experiencing?

_____

_____

_____

_____

_____

_____

_____

_____

What new experiences do I wish to create that will support more love in my life?

_____

_____

_____

_____

_____

_____

_____

_____

_____

_____

_____

_____

_____

_____

_____

_____

"Look around you, and see your world created by dreamers who began without a dollar in their bank account, yet with more passion than money could ever buy. You recognize these souls, and also realize you too can become anything your heart desires. You need only the faith to discover Source within your own soul, to provide you with all that you need to manifest that miracle."

Excerpt from Through the Eyes of Truth
A Conversation with God about My Life, Your Life, and Discovering Our Purpose

Creating Utopia
Living as a Miracle Worker Day 3

LIVING IN TRUTH

One of the most precious gifts of becoming the greatest version of yourself is that you get to create your deepest dreams without the approval from another person. How often are we reminded the only dreams that are possible are those which already exist in the world outside of us? Can you remember the last time you shared a beautiful dream you had that filled your heart with joy, only to be told that you would never achieve that dream? Either you were not wealthy enough, smart enough, or lucky enough. Yet what those people fail to realize is their opinion about your dream was never about you…. It was about them and how they perceive themselves.

You get to decide whether or not you choose to own that individuals fears or remain true to your greatest vision of what your life can become. The problem arises when we choose to adopt those fears and make them our own. The mind can only achieve what it believes, so if you choose to believe an illusion about your own self-imposed limitations, then you will create your life from those limiting thoughts.

Realize as a child of God, you have the power to create the greatest vision of your life. Nowhere in history is it stated that Source created the heavens and the earth by following another's blueprint. Since we are all extensions of Source energy and have the power to create our experiences through our thoughts, emotions, and actions then we can create our greatest vision without the understanding or the approval from another. The most important ingredient to creating your dreams is seeing your dream through the eyes of truth.

Instead of judging your own journey through the eyes of another person who is trying to understand their own, realize your truth lies within the walls of your own soul. Embrace what makes you unique and own the gifts you have been blessed with. Only then will you realize that by seeing your life through the eyes of truth, you can create that state of bliss at any moment. Embrace your truth, honor your God whisper, and create the greatest vision of your life now. Have fun and live your life as the Miracle Worker you are!

What fears have I adopted from another person(s)?"

_____

_____

_____

_____

_____

_____

_____

What can I do to listen to my voice and to my "God whisper?"

_____

_____

_____

_____

_____

_____

_____

_____

What is God whispering into my soul now about my own truth?

_____

_____

_____

_____

_____

_____

_____

_____

_____

_____

_____

_____

_____

_____

_____

_____

_____

_____

"When one soul awakens to the reality of its own perfection, a light is magnified that lights up another souls awakening. The tide of love is beyond measure. For you and I are one, and I am one with every soul you encounter. Thus in your awakening, your energy awakens another from their illusion."

Excerpt from Through the Eyes of Truth –
A Conversation with God about My Life, Your Life, and Discovering Our Purpose

Creating Utopia
Living as a Miracle Worker Day 4

SEEING BEYOND THE ILLUSION

Setting goals so often takes a large amount of faith, as we have to believe that very dream we desire to create is attainable. If we have the faith to see it in the mind's eye then we can visualize daily, connect the emotions and then our actions follow suit to create what our mind perceives. So many times we allow ourselves to dream big, only to use the same amount of energy to talk ourselves out of that dream. Think about it. As we consider the possibility of winning a competition, our emotions build and we instantly feel the excitement generated by our thoughts. Our heart begins to race and excitement wells within our spirit until suddenly the experience of winning the competition has been created in our experience.

As you hold the thoughts and emotions of already experiencing achieving your goal, then your physical body begins to change. Your heart beats faster, a smile slowly covers your face and the feelings of joy overpower your senses. Short of realizing that you are still very much in your own environment, it would appear to you that although it felt very much real, the experience was only a dream. Then as you are suddenly drawn back into your environment you realize that you were "day dreaming" and dismiss your creative abilities as just our imagination. What if your imagination was the reality and the physical environment you see with your sense was the illusion?

Maybe then you would look at all of your dreams and instead of perceiving them as impossible, they would appear to you to be the reality. You would no more wait for the approval from another person to achieve this dream than you would wait for Santa Claus to provide you with the gift you are completely capable of gifting yourself. If you begin looking at the world through the eyes of truth, then you can create utopia through any experience you have throughout your days. You are in control over your actions and reactions to your environment. If you choose to experience having a new home, then create that vision and imbed it into your soul blueprint so deep that you live, breathe and sweat that dream to the depths of your core.

You need to co-create this dream with Source energy and God is energy residing within you. Since you are the physical element of this creation then your goal is to be present in your own life moments and create them. Only then will you realize that you had the power to create the bliss and state of perfection that utopia represents to you. Realize you have the power to create the experience of your greatest dream in any situation you are experiencing this very moment. You are NOT your environment, you are NOT your family, and you are NOT your relationships. You get to create and re-create who you are every moment of your life, so choose to be in control with or without evidence of your dream.

Look at your dream as the tiny seed planted in the soil of love and nourishment. As you focus on that dream you are creating the experience of already having it even though you haven't seen the seed flourish into a lovely flower. Yet in the depths of your soul you know that through watering, attention, and nourishment, the seed will transform into a deep-rooted flower that will spring forth into the light. Right now, you are in the watering process of that tiny seed and don't need another person to give you permission to water that seed so it eventually grows into a beautiful flower. All you need is the faith to know that the more you water that seed and nurture it, you will trust that the sunlight of God will shine upon it. Then when you least expect it, you will look out of the window of your soul and see evidence of that see flourish into the beautiful flower you created. Have fun and live your life as the Miracle Worker you are!

What is my greatest dream now?

_____

_____

_____

_____

_____

_____

_____

_____

What can I do to nourish and water the seed of my dream on a daily basis?

_____

_____

_____

_____

_____

_____

_____

_____

What is God whispering into my soul now about my dream?

_____

_____

_____

_____

_____

_____

_____

_____

_____

_____

_____

_____

_____

_____

_____

_____

_____

"Everything carries with it a ripple effect. Nothing remains the same, as energy is continuously in motion. With the fervor that you send a thought and feeling out into the atmosphere, it will gain momentum and strength. When it returns to you, it is even more powerful than when you initially sent it out. You are laying the foundation and the building blocks in which your monument will not be moved. Your words and message will spread like wildfire. They will reach the smallest souls who will recognize your energy's "voice." They will trust in the truth of their own ability to create their world in the love and the light that you have created your very own."

Excerpt from Through the Eyes of Truth –
A Conversation with God about My Life, Your Life, and Discovering Our Purpose

Creating Utopia
Living as a Miracle Worker Day 5

BUILDING YOUR FOUNDATION

Faith. This is such a magical word which can mean the difference between realizing your greatest dreams or settling for creating the same experiences which fail to bring you a life of joy. Like everything in life, the foundation of any goal must be built to withstand even the darkest storms and the elements that bombard us throughout our lives. If you look at your faith as the foundation of a new house being built, then you will understand the stronger you make the foundation the more of the structure it will support. Your faith must be strong enough to withstand moments of fear and doubt so you can continue moving towards connecting to your own greatness.

How can you develop your faith to withstand the darkest clouds of fear? Through deliberately pushing yourself out of your current comfort zone so you can push beyond your current illusions of limits. First your relationship with Source lays the groundwork for your new foundation. The more you can communicate with God about your dreams the more you will understand they already exist within you. The role you play as co-creator is to connect to the Source of your dreams and build your relationship with the realization you already have what you seek.

This is where faith comes in, as you will be called upon to begin living your life and expending your energy on the truth of already seeing that dream in your reality. When we pray for a goal or a dream to be accomplished, keep in mind that Source will ask you to be a co-creator in that dream. Your role in faith is to trust in the process and understand you are building the foundation of your relationship to that dream you have yet to see. Come up with a list of things you would be doing if you already had this dream in your reality.

If you are trying to get your dream job, then write out what your responsibilities would be and how you would incorporate those responsibilities into your life today. If you are trying to obtain a healthier lifestyle, then make a list of activities and meals you would be eating today and start doing those things now. We have been trained to believe that once we see the dream manifest before our eyes, *then* we will believe it and begin acting as if it is in our reality.

The creative process is just the opposite of this illusion. You must believe in the truth that you already have your goal, your dream job, and your healthy lifestyle in your environment today and begin laying the foundation of incorporating these things into your life now. This is where faith comes in. You must desire to experience these goals in your life today, this very moment and begin laying the foundation of faith that will ultimately bring it into your fruition. Push yourself beyond your comfort zone and focus your attention on seeing what you know to be truth and you will see the vision of your greatest life grow more evident in your reality. Have fun and live your life as the Miracle Worker you are!

What can I do to strengthen my foundation of faith?

_____

_____

_____

_____

_____

_____

_____

What daily actions can I take to strengthen my faith in the creation of my dreams?

_____

_____

_____

_____

_____

_____

_____

What is God whispering into my soul now about my dream?

_____

_____

_____

_____

_____

_____

_____

_____

_____

_____

_____

_____

_____

_____

_____

_____

_____

"Yet so many souls fail to pray correctly, because they seek to find peace. Yet when they have to turn their attention inwards to the perfection of their own souls, it makes them so uncomfortable that they cannot hold their attention long enough to hear my answer. Rarely are the answers to your prayers in the form of a simple yes, no, or not now. Again, when you have a conversation with your parent, child or spouse, are you only answering in one-sentence answers? Then how is it that you believe your Creator and the purest source of love in your life would answer you any differently?"

Excerpt from Through the Eyes of Truth –
A Conversation with God about My Life, Your Life, and Discovering Our Purpose

Creating Utopia
Living as a Miracle Worker Day 6

WHO HEARS YOU?

Let me ask you something...when you pray, do you believe that Source hears you? Before you continue reading this, answer this question and just sit for a moment and allow this to resonate with you. Do you believe God hears your every prayer and is waiting attentively to answer back to you? If so, then proceed. If not, then ask yourself why you feel so unworthy as to think for a moment that God doesn't hear your voice. After all, if you are co-creating your life with Source then you must believe you are connected to a level of pure love.

It's interesting to me that we are taught from a young age to believe in a benevolent and loving God, yet at the same time are told if we do anything wrong then this same loving God will banish us into an eternal nightmare. How can we then not help but feel unworthy or underserving of God's love? When we adopt these illusions that we somehow have to succumb to conditional love in our Creators life, then we take this unworthiness and create more experiences that create feelings of unworthiness.

One of those experiences is through our communication with God. We are not sure how to pray and even more unsure as to the manner in which Source communicates with us. Because of this we feel uneasy about prayer and establishing our relationship with God. Allowing yourself to release all the illusions you have adopted about Source and seek your own personal relationship with God in the manner you desire to have it. Then you will be able to ask God for guidance in building the connection to your greatest dreams.

Utilize your internal GPS and ask Source for specific guidance while creating the greatest version of yourself. If your dream resides deep in the corners of your mind, then give yourself permission to release it and while you are creating it, you will learn faith at a greater level than you have known before. Your faith will be called forth as you are focusing your own thoughts, emotions, and actions on creating the experience of already having your dream. During this process you are also building your connection with Source and you will learn to identify the voice of God within you. This allows you to establish your own relationship with Source and know without a shadow of a doubt that your voice is being heard in prayer.

Also know that communication is a two-way street, so as you are calling out to God then expect Source to answer you as well. Sit still in silence and trust the information you are receiving. You will be led to create your greatest dreams that you once thought were impossible. Since you have free will then realize you will be called on to do something as well to create your dreams. Your role is to trust the process, ask God for guidance, and know that all miracles reside within you. Have fun and live your life as the Miracle Worker you are!

Do I believe God hears my prayers? Why or why not?

_____

_____

_____

_____

_____

_____

_____

_____

What can I do to hear God's whisper and how can I establish a deeper relationship with God?

_____

_____

_____

_____

_____

_____

_____

_____

What is God whispering into my soul now about our relationship?

_____

_____

_____

_____

_____

_____

_____

_____

_____

_____

_____

_____

_____

_____

_____

_____

_____

"Use not the illusions of time or lack in which to deny yourself any longer. I tell you this, through denying self, you are denying uplifting another. You are responsible for your own gifts. By sharing them with yourself, you share them in turn with the light of souls around you. Instead seek to fulfill a purpose greater than yourself. Look to Source within for the courage to guide you where you need to go."

Excerpt from Through the Eyes of Truth –
A Conversation with God about My Life, Your Life, and Discovering Our Purpose

Creating Utopia
Living as a Miracle Worker Day 7

WRITE YOUR STORY

When it comes to the power of creation, we have only to understand that we are creating every moment in our lives. Although we cannot control how other people treat us or circumstances out of our control, we can control how we react to these experiences. Every moment in our life we have the power to create from the two most powerful creative forces – love or fear. Love creates emotions of joy, empowerment, euphoria, etc. and fear creates anger, resentment, jealousy, and many other negative emotions.

We must empower ourselves by realizing we can choose what emotions we wish to experience throughout our days. Through those emotions we then choose the corresponding thoughts and actions to support our physical experiences. However, if we have spent the majority of our lives creating from a place of fear then we tend to continue manifesting experiences that will support our comfortable emotions of fear. We need to become aware of not only how we think but how we choose to feel every moment of our lives because these are the moments of creation.

Ask yourself how you can create new experiences through your emotions and what you can do to create a life of purpose that supports emotions of love and joy. By doing a "spirit check" throughout the day, you are shifting your energy to be proactive rather than reactive. Think about it, wouldn't you rather experience feelings of being happy rather than feelings of being angry or insecure? The root of our thoughts are connected to the emotions we are most comfortable having in our life.

As a child of God and a co-creator in your life journey, you have the free will to choose what emotions you experience throughout the day. Granted, life often throws us some curve balls and it is difficult if not seemingly impossible to force yourself to experience joy when you are struggling through difficult life circumstances. However, you know how you think and feel, and allowing yourself to experience the feelings of fear as you transition slowly into emotions of comfort and love will come from the power of prayer. Always trust you are connected to something greater than yourself. Know that voice in your spirit which brings you love and comforts your moments of fear is as real as you are. Most importantly never allow yourself to believe the illusion you are not worthy of having all your heart desires. You are a child of God and abundance of everything your soul desires to experience is your birthright. Now live your life as the Miracle Worker you are!

What patterns of emotions have I become comfortable experiencing?

_____

_____

_____

_____

_____

_____

_____

What can I do to be more proactive in how I choose to feel throughout the day?

_____

_____

_____

_____

_____

_____

_____

_____

What is God whispering into my soul and how do I feel when I hear my God whisper?

_____

_____

_____

_____

_____

_____

_____

_____

_____

_____

_____

_____

_____

_____

_____

_____

_____

_____

_____

"You are chosen to create a path that is yours alone. It cannot be sought with the guidance and approval from the world around you. The desire you have, combined with the love in which you seek it will bring the road to your vision. Suddenly doubt and fear will be removed and the illusion of fog will lift to reveal a path so extraordinary, you will revel in the journey with me. You will seek only truth from my guidance. Your fear will transform into courage to complete what your soul desired to create before your existence in the physical plane."

Excerpt from Creating Utopia –
Living Life as a Miracle Worker

Creating Utopia
Living as a Miracle Worker Day 8

YOU ARE CHOSEN

Every day I work with some of the most amazing women in the world, and one of the consistent illusions I have discovered, is that we fail to acknowledge our own worthiness. As children of God, we are deserving of being loved, respected and filled with joy. As a matter of fact, abundance of everything that brings us love is not only our inheritance but our birthright! How then do so many of us lack the self-love to receive our own gifts as well as love from others? Why do so many beautiful souls feel unworthy of being loved?

If you only understood that part of the creative process is not only creating our gifts from love but receiving them from love as well, we may be more apt to want to love ourselves. We seem to have the hardest time grasping the concept that we are chosen by God and through God to inherit our kingdom, but we need to first be willing to receive it in the love it was intended. Why does Source have to spend so much energy attempting to convince us that we are deserving of having abundance of love and joy in our lives?

Yet rather than understanding we need to embrace our own perfection in order to receive our gifts, we spend more time trying to earn love from the world around us. Somehow many have bought into the illusion that we need to earn love in order to love ourselves. If we each can take time every day learning to appreciate ourselves for being the amazing souls that we are, I feel we would judge others less and embrace ourselves more. Our greatest responsibility is to love ourselves first and then learn to share that love with the world around us. However, many people are putting others before them and never allowing themselves to receive their own gift of self-love.

What would you do if God spoke to you and told you that you were chosen for something so perfect, only you could create the miracle? How would you respond when you hear the voice of your Creator speaking truth into your soul, and asking you to embrace your own greatness in order to accept your highest calling? Would you honor your God whisper, or would you look for approval in the world outside of you? If you envision seeking the approval from your God whisper from the world outside of you, then you may never truly embrace your own magical journey.

Unleash your self-imposed limitations and replace them with the gifts of a sound heart, mind, and body. Allow yourself the courtesy to receive your own love in the same magnitude you share that love with the world outside of you. When you learn to embrace yourself on every level, you will understand what it is to be one with your Creator. Then receiving the love through waves of miracles Source has created for you will seem as easy as loving yourself. Ask yourself, what will you do when you hear the call from God, asking you to embrace your own perfection? Now is the time to honor your calling and receive the gifts of miracles you have awaiting you!

"My child you have come to the intersection where your illusion has met your truth. You are at the point of illusion and utopia, and must be deliberate in the direction you wish to continue your journey. As you stand at the crossroads of life you get to choose as to how you will co-create your life. Do you desire to create a life of love and joy from using your spiritual gifts and honoring your calling? Or would you prefer to continue navigating blindly down the path where many walk while having no loving direction or purpose? Your soul has brought you to this intersection so you can make a conscious choice as to how you are going to create the life of your dreams."

Excerpt from Creating Utopia –
Living Life as a Miracle Worker

Creating Utopia
Living as a Miracle Worker Day 9

THE INTERSECTION OF ILLUSION AND UTOPIA (DENIABILITY AND ACCOUNTABILITY)

The act of prayer is a conversation between Source and ourselves. Through the interaction of asking and waiting for a response, we learn to tune into the voice of God and tune out the noise of the world around us. Through my personal prayers and learning that I can define my relationship with Source to the extent that I want to experience it, I know that I must be open to receiving my answers to my own prayers. When we have a conversation with anyone, we know that in order to have a mutually beneficial conversation we must learn to speak and when to listen. I think we often forget to listen when we speak to God.

As co-creators in our own lives, we have the free will to choose our thoughts, emotions, and subsequently our actions. We can create the same old patterns that no longer serve us, or we can choose to create new patterns that will bring about the creation of new experiences. In order to use the power of free will we were granted, we should remember that when we call upon God for the creation of a "miracle," we must remember that Source will call upon us to follow through on our own creative energy as well. God won't force us to act in a particular way if we are in charge of our own body, mind, and spirit.

However, I believe that God will guide us to move in a certain direction while speaking to our spirit and serving as a guidance system towards creating a new path. What happens though when we are called upon to begin a new creation, is that we often resist the discomfort of the new feelings and resort back into our old limiting thoughts. We ask God to create a chance to empower ourselves as co-creators through winning a competition, yet when God asks us to begin new thoughts, emotions, and actions that support this creation in our lives, we resist. Why? Because we have believed an illusion that we must first see the evidence of that very thing we are creating before we believe it exists.

However, if we are co-creating our lives with God, then we must be accountable for the creation of what we are capable of manifesting. We must first create the experience of already having that very thing we desire in our lives in order to see the evidence of it in our reality. In order to do this, we must realize our own choices create our experiences. When we stand at the corner of accountability and denial, we must remind ourselves that we are responsible for creating that very experience we are praying to God for. Then we must choose to be accountable for walking in faith and only seeing the evidence of that very thing we are praying for.

If we choose not to be accountable, then we are in fact denying ourselves the experience of creating that very miracle we are asking Source for. If our prayer includes that God's will be done, then we must understand on a soul level we are also accountable for being part of the miracle that creates the miracle. So, the next time you stand at the intersection of accountability and denial, what road will you choose to travel? Uttering the words in prayer, "may thy will be done," will often lead to the response, "then choose thy will and it will be done." Enjoy your life, have fun, and live your life as the Miracle Worker God created you to be! Your journey begins with a prayer.

What choices am I not taking accountability for in my life?

_____

_____

_____

_____

_____

_____

_____

What can I do to receive my gifts rather than deny myself my gifts of self-love?

_____

_____

_____

_____

_____

_____

_____

What is God whispering into my soul about receiving self-love?

_____

_____

_____

_____

_____

_____

_____

_____

_____

_____

_____

_____

_____

_____

_____

_____

_____

"Would you not agree that the physical and the spiritual journey are one when you are in the vehicle of your physical body? Your body rarely embarks on a journey without your mind first navigating the safest and most direct and enjoyable route. Yet you would rather neglect your own soul than to risk listening to my whispers echoing throughout the walls of your truth. If you continue to follow your physical senses and convince yourself that is all there is, then you will continue to neglect your own soul and put your journey with me on autopilot."

Excerpt from Creating Utopia –
Living Life as a Miracle Worker

Creating Utopia
Living as a Miracle Worker Day 10

BEING AS ONE WITH YOUR CREATOR

So often when we are attempting to create miracles in our own lives, we perceive the goal as being separate from us. It is almost as if we are trying to reach for something outside of us rather than tap into the magic within us. Remembering that our connection to reality and to God lies within us, we must continually reach for the connection to our experience within our own souls. Then the perception of separateness dissolves and is replaced by unity with Source.

Learning how to change our perspective assists us in understanding the world of illusion. So often we tend to see our lives through one set of lenses, and the perspective is one of separateness. What if we could change our perspective and rather than viewing everything outside of us, we see ourselves in the experience? For instance, take something as beautiful as a flower. When you first glance at a lovely flower you notice the beauty through color. If you study that flower longer then you become aware of the fragrance the flower is releasing and as you breathe that flower into your own senses, you grow more connected to it. Then you touch the flower and sense the lush petals underneath your fingertips, which creates within you an emotion as well.

Rather than turning your attention away from the flower, now see it for its essence and its perfection. The more you connect with this flower the less of a separation you feel from it. This is the same for any experience you wish to have, as you are one with God and Source is one with all there is. Knowing this, wouldn't it be more effective searching for the experience within your soul rather than outside of your physical body?

Of course, you must do more than merely dream about your ultimate goal, as you need to use all of your creative energy to manifest that very experience you desire to have in your life. Thoughts, emotions, and actions all connect to the experience of creation, so while you are sitting in front of the television eating chocolates and doing nothing to strengthen and tone your boy, you won't be creating your ultimate healthy lifestyle.

You need to search within for the connection to the healthy and active lifestyle you wish to have and then think like a healthy person, create emotional patterns that support your desire to empower yourself and ultimately move your body towards adopting healthier eating and exercise habits that will support your goals. Realize that you have the ability to tap into your greatest resource through the power of prayer and the power of your own creative energy. Create your miracles and live your life as a Miracle Worker!

What goal do I want to create in my life?

_____

_____

_____

_____

_____

_____

_____

What can I do to create the connection of already having that goal in my existence?

_____

_____

_____

_____

_____

_____

_____

_____

What is God whispering into my soul about my unity with my desired goal?

_____

_____

_____

_____

_____

_____

_____

_____

_____

_____

_____

_____

_____

_____

_____

_____

_____

"As I watch you stand in awe of the possibilities of your choices, I am still so connected to you, yet you fail to see me. You have forgotten that I have been a part of you since your inception. I will never be apart from you other than through your illusion of creating separateness. I plead to you my child to take notice of the signs I have given you that remind you of a journey you created so long ago. A journey only you can walk through faith and courage. Although I am very much a part of you, I cannot take control over your direction because we agreed you would have free will to create your life as you please. I honor this vow every moment I watch you create a life of fear. Now I desire only that you take notice of me and hear my voice echoing through the walls of your soul. Do you hear me?"

__Excerpt from Creating Utopia –__
__Living Life as a Miracle Worker__

Creating Utopia
Living as a Miracle Worker Day 11

HONORING YOUR SIGNS

From an early age we are taught to become aware of signs around us. These signs that warn us of impending danger, slows us down, stops us, and even directs us in the right direction of our journey. These signs are all around us and without them, we would be walking through a world filled with chaos. More importantly we would fail to follow our path due to lack of understanding what road we are to take that will lead us to our final destination.

So often what we fail to realize is that God is sending us signs continually, yet we fail to recognize them. Why? When did we learn that the only signs we are to follow are the physical signs that inform us to *Stop, Yield,* or *Proceed with Caution*? If we can learn to trust our intuition and our God whisper, then we become more aware of the signs all around us. Those same signals that warn us about a particular person or situation that doesn't serve our greater good or those opportunities we are to take because God has something special planned just for us.

Just through the miracles I have witnessed throughout my life, I know that Source has provided me and continues to lead me through obvious signs along my journey. I call them my "burning bushes" and they have always led me to my greater truth. Yet I feel that we are also called to walk through these roads in faith and courage, because we have yet to see the bigger picture of what is being created before our very eyes. If we can exercise our faith daily and learn to tap into our own soul, then our journey will lead us towards a greater truth of who we are.

Look back at your life and ask yourself how many times you had the opportunity to honor your "signs" yet you chose the path of the world of illusion. Just because it seemed more real to you does not in fact mean that it is. Listen to your heart and meditate in prayer on a daily basis. Then you will discover your connection to God and your ultimate destiny lies not in the hands of another person, but in the power of your own choices to create a bond nothing can break apart.

Look at your world and ask yourself what signs you have been ignoring. Are there any wonders and "coincidences" that you have neglected because you were in fear of following? I have learned that we often tend to fear the unknown, and if God is asking you to walk through an open door with nothing more than a bag filled with faith, then leave the remaining baggage at the door and walk through the new door of opportunity. Trust that you will be led through love and joy while discovering a journey unlike any other.

We are all connected to God and as one with Source, we have only to trust our signs and honor our God whisper. Then will we know what it is to discover a world unlike any other. One where miracles are created through love and grace, and through the power of our own divine connection. Enjoy your precious life and continue to create miracles and live your life as a Miracle Worker!

What signs have I noticed in my life?

_____

_____

_____

_____

_____

_____

_____

_____

Why am I in fear of following these God sings?

_____

_____

_____

_____

_____

_____

_____

_____

What is God whispering into my soul about my signs leading towards my desired goal?

_____

_____

_____

_____

_____

_____

_____

_____

_____

_____

_____

_____

_____

_____

_____

_____

_____

"As you identify your fears, your dream becomes an even greater possibility. For it is already alive within you and has been seeking you as much as you have been seeking it. There is nothing you can do to separate yourself from your greatest vision except through your own perception of not having it. Alter your perspective and the world around you will appear different than it has before. Identify your fears and understand by holding on to that which brings fear and anxiety into your heart, you alone are keeping the fear alive. You must change your perspective, and realize the familiar emotions of fear prevent the new emotions of love from uniting as one."

Excerpt from Creating Utopia –
Living Life as a Miracle Worker

Creating Utopia
Living as a Miracle Worker Day 12

FACING YOUR FEARS

It often intrigues me that although our soul knows the road we follow to our greater purpose is filled with less people, our ego still thinks it needs the approval from more people. I often tell my clients that when you are called to follow the path of your own greater journey, you will more than likely walk that path feeling alone but never lonely. As we tune out the noise of the world and tune into the voice of God, it becomes easier to listen with our entire being. In other words, we are less distracted and more connected to truth. As a result we walk our path with fewer people guiding us and being in tuned to our internal God whisper.

I beileve that part of our fear lies in the fear of the unknown as well as in our lack of feeling worthy to receive all that God has planned for us. As we walk through the same patterns in life, repeating the same habits that create our days and the foundation of our relationships, we often fail to notice the small things that bring us the greatest fears. We listen more to the opinions of our friends and well-meaning relatives who insist that we are to do the same things because they are afraid for us.

After all, it isn't any fun having your heart broken due to not accomplishing a lofty goal. Somehow we believe an illusion that it is somehow more bearable to grieve everyday for the emptiness of trying to accomplish a goal rather than try and not achieve that goal. At some point in our lives, we must take accountability for our own actions and ask ourselves why we choose to live daily with an aching heart that desires so much to use our own creative energy to manifest a life of joy. How can we convince ourselves that it is somehow easier to ache daily than to experience the joy and love from self as we figure out ways to accomplish what others may deem "miracles."

Everyday we choose to live out our lives through the eyes of doubt and fear rather than through the eyes of truth and love, is another day that we choose not to be connected to Source on a greater level. Nobody can convince me that it is safer for me to sit back and watch my life happen through the opinion of another person. I would always rather be the one person in the corner of the world trying to find new ways to achieve greater possibilities... wouldn't you? If I fail at my first attempt then I get up and continue trying new and unique ways to create joy and self-love in my own life. This way I will never look back on my life with regret and wonder, "what if."

Ask yourself, "what if I wasn't too old to achieve my dream?" "What if I was only one thought and action away from manifesting the greatest vision of my life today?" Most importantly, "what if all of these efforts led me to know, love, and honor myself and my Creator to a level I never thought possible?" Stop living your life through the illusion of fear and choose to be a deliberate co-creator in your own life. After all, OWN and WON are two magnificent words in only 3 letters. The moment you own your dream is the moment you won your greatest goal! Now live your life as the miracle workers you are and keep reaching for the world of possibilities!

What fears am I creating daily in my own life?

_____

_____

_____

_____

_____

_____

_____

How can I change my perception of these illusions and exchange fear for love?

_____

_____

_____

_____

_____

_____

_____

What is God whispering into my soul about releasing my fears and reaching for my dreams?

_____

_____

_____

_____

_____

_____

_____

_____

_____

_____

_____

_____

_____

_____

_____

_____

_____

"What often separates you from your desired dream is not the fact that it has yet to be created, rather you have yet to connect yourself to what has already been created by you and for you. My child, you live in an illusion filled universe where you have convinced yourself of the falsehood, that if you do not see the dream in front of you then it has yet to exist. In fact, the opposite is true. Your dream already exists and is very much alive, yet your role is to align yourself with that dream and already see it within your life. Then your perspective will shift from not having to already having that which you desire to create. Nothing separates you from your dreams greater than fear and the illusion of time."

Excerpt from Creating Utopia –
Living Life as a Miracle Worker

Creating Utopia
Living as a Miracle Worker Day 13

THE ILLUSION OF TIME AND SEPARATION

So many of us have learned to only believe in what we see, rather than what we know we are capable of creating. Because of this, we tend to remain fixated on the illusion of separation from our dreams rather than the reality that our dreams already exist within us. Rather than choosing to live in the experience of joy and gratitude, we tend to live in the emotions of fear and anxiety. If we have but two emotions to use in the creative process, then we have the free will to choose exactly what emotion we are creating our lives through.

Take for instance the creation of fear. This often leads to the perception that we are somehow separate from our own dreams and greatest goals. Rather than viewing the creative process through our entire being, we witness it through only one set of lenses…. through our physical eyes. Then if we fail to see our dream in front of us, we will continue convincing ourselves that it doesn't yet exist. What then happens is that we look for the dream outside of us through seeking permission from others to give it to us.

However, when we shift our perspective and choose to see our greatest dream through our minds eye, then we are able to take a step away from the physical and witness the manifestation of that dream within. As our observation grows, we then become more aware of the presence of our goal and the feeling of excitement it brings into your life. Your heart beats a little faster and your body gets covered in chills through the awareness of its presence already within you. The more you focus on the emotions of experiencing the goal, the less aware you are of the illusion that it doesn't exist.

As you open your eyes, remain fixed on the feeling of joy and gratitude your connection to your dream has created within you. Be sure not to shift your awareness of its separation from you through or you will need to reconnect with the process of connection once again. Then you become aware that your dream doesn't become separated from you through time or space, because you were able to experience the creation of its existence within you just moments ago. Continue seeing the bigger picture of your greatest dream and remain connected to the experience of already having it. Then you will realize nothing separates you from the experience of creating it.

Live each day as a Miracle Worker and continue having fun creating the life of your dreams. This is the only life you have so celebrate in your creation of it through the power of prayer and the power of God!

What perception do I have of competition when it comes to creating my dreams?

_____

_____

_____

_____

_____

_____

_____

How can I change my perception of separation of time and distance from my dream?

_____

_____

_____

_____

_____

_____

_____

_____

What is God whispering into my soul about already having my dreams in my reality?

_____

_____

_____

_____

_____

_____

_____

_____

_____

_____

_____

_____

_____

_____

_____

_____

_____

_____

_____

_____

"Trust your intuition when it comes to creation and seek to know yourself before you adopt another soul's fear. For I bring you glimpses of what is possible for you to create, so you can become inspired and transform your own life in the greatest form that brings you love and joy. Cease from seeking validation from anyone outside of you, for within your own soul lies a miracle just waiting to happen. You are the creator of your dreams and have only to tap into your own power to create the vision of love in your life. This is why it is so important that you first seek your truth through prayer and I will guide you to the waters of life. I will reveal to you the power you have to create anything your heart desires to experience through the power of your own intention."

Excerpt from Creating Utopia –
Living Life as a Miracle Worker

Creating Utopia
Living as a Miracle Worker Day 14

LISTEN TO YOUR INTUITION

Although we often find it difficult to create new patterns of thinking and acting in our own lives, we also realize we need to do different things in order to get different results. An effective method I have learned to use is to trust my intuition and listen to my God whisper. By developing a relationship with Source we learn to have a prayer and a conversation with God. One that allows us to ask questions or just to listen to our God whisper and understand a level of truth unlike any other. When we listen to our intuition then we develop a level of faith that is peaceful within our spirit. It allows us to understand on a soul level the difference between truth and illusion lies in our perception of it.

Then we can begin asking questions on a level of truth we never fully embraced. Questions such as, how can we connect to our dream within so we can experience it in the world outside of us. When we connect with Source and have these conversations with God, we learn the dream already exists within us. Our role is to vibrate on the same frequency of this dream so we can feel it alive within us. When this happens then our emotions feel the excitement of already having our dream in our life and it begins to feel real to us. The more you can align your actions with supporting the evidence of the dream already in your life, the more you connect to that dream and bring it to life.

Trust your own song and listen only to the guidance coming from within your own soul whispers when it comes to creating miracles in your life. Instead what often happens is that we seek the support from others around us to sustain our faith rather than seeking the support from God. It is almost as if we fear our own greatness in being able to achieve our greatest goals. Then we would have to justify to others why God felt us worthy to create the life of our dreams when in fact we need to see ourselves worthy of receiving love from Source. There are so many people who convince themselves they would rather deal with the daily disappointment of not reaching their greatest dreams rather than with the heartbreak of not achieving their goal if they tried.

Either way your heart is breaking, so wouldn't you rather take the risk of empowering yourself by trying daily to be a greater version of who you are meant to be? Taking control of manifesting your greatest dreams one step at a time is one tool for empowerment and living your life as the child of God you are. Learn to tap into your intuition and establish your own conversations with God so you know your guidance is coming from Source. Have faith in the unseen and realize at any given point in your life, you can connect with your greatest dreams through your own creative power.

Live your life, celebrate the amazing person you are and continue creating miracles your own life one day at a time. Live, love, and laugh Miracle Workers!

Do I trust my own intuition and my inner God whisper?

_____

_____

_____

_____

_____

_____

_____

How can I become a greater version of myself through my own intuition?

_____

_____

_____

_____

_____

_____

_____

What is God whispering into my soul today through my intuition and my God whisper?

_____

_____

_____

_____

_____

_____

_____

_____

_____

_____

_____

_____

_____

_____

_____

_____

_____

_____

"So much of the world today is filled with a sense of entitlement and not purpose. You seek the grandest expression of yourself outside of you rather than create it first from within. So now I ask you, what is it you seek to give of yourself in order to create love in its purest form? What gift from your soul are you willing to develop in order for another to know the love of God and love of self?"

Excerpt from Creating Utopia –
Living Life as a Miracle Worker

Creating Utopia
Living as a Miracle Worker Day 15

WHAT WILL YOU CONTRIBUTE?

Ask yourself one question. While you are in the journey into self-discovery as a creator of your life, "what do I want to share with the world around me?" After all, if we are all created by one omnipotent Source and we are all one with God, then wouldn't it make sense that we are all one with each other? Yes, we are all experiencing this life through separate bodies and minds, but what if our souls are all connected in some way through the power of God? Would it make a difference in how you want to connect with your purpose and live your passion?

When God provides us with gifts, we are inspired to create our lives through them because it brings us closer to love. What if these gifts also brought others somehow closer to their own purpose through our divine connection? When I hear a beautiful singer, I get chills throughout my entire body and feel the love and passion from that person flow through my veins. When I watch something that warms my heart, it brings me to tears because I feel the joy the author is sharing from their soul to mine. What gifts do you have that will not only inspire your own life but create a ripple effect of inspiration to the world around you?

If we asked ourselves this question before we set our own self-imposed limitations, then we may be able to rise above the limiting patterns we have set in our own life. Maybe we would look for ways to accomplish the "unattainable" or soar beyond the "disability" that society has created a label for. When we choose to see ourselves through the eyes of truth then we are more willing to take the leap of faith that many would scoff at. Only because it has yet to be done, not because it is unattainable.

What if you choose to wake up every morning and rather than live your life through a set of limiting patterns, chose to create a brand new miracle in your life? Then the world would soon discover that we only perceive life as either limitations or miracles. There are so many people creating their life dreams through living a life of purpose and passion. What will you do to create yours? When God knocks on the door of your soul tonight in a beautiful dream, how will you respond? Will you gather one bag that carries your passions, purpose, and miracles? Or will you make excuses because you are choosing to carry too much baggage of burdens from illusions you chose to adopt? The choice is yours Miracle Worker... it's all yours.

Do I know my God given gifts? What are they and how do I feel when I perform them?

_____

_____

_____

_____

_____

_____

_____

What gifts do I have that can inspire or empower another person? How?

_____

_____

_____

_____

_____

_____

_____

What is God whispering into my soul today about creating and sharing my gifts?

_____

_____

_____

_____

_____

_____

_____

_____

_____

_____

_____

_____

_____

_____

_____

_____

_____

"Far too often however, souls will distance themselves from the outcome they desire because they believe that joy is a destination. Joy is a state of being. Until you understand this, you will continue placing conditions on being joyous. For instance, so many of you say that you will be happy when you lose weight, you will be happy when you find the partner of your dreams, or you will be happy when you get a new home. Realize as joy is a state of being, you need not place the illusion of time into the creation of that joy you desire to experience. You can create it now at this very moment by placing your mind and heart into a state of being joyous."

Excerpt from Creating Utopia –
Living Life as a Miracle Worker

Creating Utopia
Living as a Miracle Worker Day 16

JOY IS NOT A DESTINATION

When we think about creating our greatest vision of our lives, we immediately experience the joy of already having that goal in our reality. The feeling of bliss fills our hearts and our energy begins to change from separation of our goal to already having the experience of it now. Consider how this joy brought you so much peace and gratitude, and then open your eyes and look at the environment you are currently in. Do you remain connected to your emotions of joy, or is your immediate thought disappointment and separation from your goal?

Realizing the joy, you just experienced moments ago was very much a real sensation, you become aware that joy is not a place or a time. Joy is an emotion that allows you the connection between you and your desired goal to be one in thought and emotion. By remembering that you bring in your desired goal into your life through your own creative process, you can change your perspective from being separate from that goal to already having it. This is why competition is such a mental game of creation and is often "won" first in the mind. Understanding how the creative process works allows you to experience the creation of that very goal you are bringing into your reality now. You learn to be joyous in the moment of creation which is the moment of connection for you.

Then through repetition of your connection through thoughts and emotions, you begin acting as if the experience is already in your life. This brings about more feelings of joy and gratitude until your mind and goal are one and the same. Remember there is no separation from your "miracle" except through your perception of separateness. When you feel isolated from your goal then you lose the feelings of joy that you are meant to have. Find ways to reconnect with your joy through daily meditations and visualizations. Then follow through with action that supports your desired outcome, so every day you are working towards creating your goals whether they are creating a healthier body or creating your dream house for your family.

Life is a beautiful journey that is meant to be celebrated on all levels. Find joy in your life in every moment so you can continue being the wonderful Miracle Workers in your own life that God intended you to be. Always remember you are one with Source and nothing can separate you from the love of God, so enjoy the journey.

Do I know my God given gifts? What are they and how do I feel when I perform them?

_____

_____

_____

_____

_____

_____

_____

What gifts do I have that can inspire or empower another person? How?

_____

_____

_____

_____

_____

_____

_____

_____

What is God whispering into my soul today about creating and sharing my gifts?

_____

_____

_____

_____

_____

_____

_____

_____

_____

_____

_____

_____

_____

_____

_____

_____

_____

_____

_____

_____

"For your dreams are not separate from you, nor do they have the power to exist without your observation and interpretation of them. As nothing exists in your reality without first you being the creator and the observer. Knowing this, how have you justified that your dreams were taken by another due to someone or something keeping you from experiencing them? Yet so many magnificent souls choose to disempower themselves by blaming their lack of accomplishing goals on something outside of their control."

Excerpt from Creating Utopia –
Living Life as a Miracle Worker

Creating Utopia
Living as a Miracle Worker Day 17

REFLECTIONS OF GRACE

How many times throughout your life have you talked yourself out of pursuing a lofty goal because you lacked the faith to believe it was possible to achieve? Now ask yourself how many times you have ceased from creating the greatest dream you have because you felt you were not worthy enough to receive it? If you think about both of these examples, they always come down to us being in complete control of stopping the creation of our dream before it is even manifested. What's worse it that we create patterns of giving up on our dreams before we know what it feels like to actually accomplish it. In other words, we become creators of setting experiences that bring the emotions of disappointing ourselves rather than empowering ourselves.

If we could only stop and look at ourselves through the eyes of truth, we would see God's reflection staring back at us. How can our Creator find us so worthy, yet we fail to recognize that same value in our own eyes? I believe that in any moment, God sends us reflections of grace. Those moments when we receive confirmation we are on the right path towards our greatest journey through a stranger's kind words or a sign we see along our day. I believe these moments of grace are God's way of igniting that spark within us so we can continue believing in the unseen. Continue believing in ourselves.

We look at the world outside of us and often seek our validation and approval from others. What we often fail to realize is that this world is filled with dreamers who have allowed fear to overtake their love for their own dream. Then we seek approval from these same people who have lacked recognizing value in themselves so they share the same fears with us. Rather than question the foundation by which these people have built their lives, we immediately choose to believe and adopt their fears and make them our own.

If we can find moments along our path to recognize and be in gratitude for our reflections of truth, then I believe we will continue moving forward towards our greatest dreams by looking only into the eyes of God rather than the eyes of fear. Ask yourself what dreams you have ignored because you failed to recognize your own reflections of grace. How have you chosen to ignore the voice of truth and adopted another person's fear? Most importantly, how can you shift your awareness from the eyes of fear to the eyes of truth so you can connect with your dream once again?

This life is but a short and magical journey, and you can ride the rollercoaster of joy or fear. Seize every moment and look for opportunities to connect with Source and there you will discover your greatest dream is just a moment away. Continue living your life as Miracle Workers and your will continue creating more miracles.

What have been some moments when I noticed God confirming my dreams?

_____

_____

_____

_____

_____

_____

_____

How can I change my perspective to recognize these moments of grace?

_____

_____

_____

_____

_____

_____

_____

_____

What is God whispering into my soul today about my greatest dreams?

_____

_____

_____

_____

_____

_____

_____

_____

_____

_____

_____

_____

_____

_____

_____

_____

_____

"Since you and I are one and I am one with all there is, realize there is no separation between you and this dream. Connecting to my love and experiencing the peace and joy of already being one with your dream will in fact connect you to this greater than anything else you can do. As you use your creative power through your thoughts that bring in the detailed vision of already having this, you are creating the connection between you and that which you desire. Replace the fear with love and you will experience only love for this new dream."

Excerpt from Creating Utopia –
Living Life as a Miracle Worker

Creating Utopia
Living as a Miracle Worker Day 18

SEPARATION OF JOY AND FEAR

We are not our bodies and we are not our condition. We are spirits of perfection having an experience in our physical body. This is such an important truth to remember, because as spirit beings having a physical experience we tend to place conditions on ourselves that are so powerful, we create our lives from those emotions. At any point in our lives we have the choice to create our lives through emotions of love or fear.

What happens is that as creatures of habit, our illusion will never change until our perception of it changes. In other words, when we choose to create our life experiences from a condition outside of ourselves then we have disconnected ourselves from being co-creators in our own lives. When we say to ourselves that we will be happy when we lose 10 pounds or we will be happy only when we have the perfect life partner, then we convince ourselves to believe that our joy lies in a condition.

Rather than trying to change the condition (which is a complete illusion by the way) and placing our joy on those illusions, we need to change our perspective. Look at your life through creating with two emotions: love or fear. It is that simple except the work comes in forcing ourselves every moment to do a spirit check and create our life through the emotions of love. Having that separation between joy and fear allows us to simplify our options and know we can change our perspective to choose love and joy and suddenly our energy changes to be more joyous.

I have a dear friend who has become my accountability partner to help me shift my old patterns of fear into love. Every morning we text one another those things in our lives we are joyous and in gratitude for. It forces us to begin the day being in joy. If one or the other of us fails to send the text, we remind one another to change our thoughts and follow through. It becomes much easier to have someone else to partner with so we don't fall back into old patterns of fear. Make a choice every moment of your life to be aware of how you are creating your life, and live your precious life through the emotions of love and joy.

Continue creating what the world would consider to be a miracle and you will continue creating more miracles to be in gratitude for. Live life to the fullest and find ways to become a better version of yourself so you will always receive the abundance of love and dreams you are worthy of. Here is to you Miracle Workers!

How am I celebrating my greatest joy?

_____

_____

_____

_____

_____

_____

_____

What are my greatest fears? How do I create patterns that bring more fear into my life?

_____

_____

_____

_____

_____

_____

_____

What is God whispering into my soul about my joys and how can I create more joy?

_____

_____

_____

_____

_____

_____

_____

_____

_____

_____

_____

_____

_____

_____

_____

_____

_____

_____

"Follow the song in your heart and know that another has placed the melody there to remind you of your own greatness. If a beautiful melody is playing in the corner of your soul and you hear it not, how will you know the sounds of beauty you can express through the power of creation?"

**Excerpt from Creating Utopia –
Living Life as a Miracle Worker**

Creating Utopia
Living as a Miracle Worker Day 19

HEARING THE MELODY OF YOUR OWN SONG

As a coach who gets to work with women across the world, I am in awe of the amazing souls God continues to send my way. Whether I am coaching a young woman in India, Australia, Great Britain, Japan, or somewhere in the USA, I have found the same repeating theme in all women. We have a desire to live a life of purpose and discover our passion. We know there is something greater we have to offer and our heart yearns for the connection to something or somebody greater than ourselves to help us find that purpose.

Yet what I have discovered is that so many of us have lost the song of our heart along the road of life. At some point in our journey through this illusion filled life, we chose to believe a lie that our song was not worthy of being played. We were convinced that another person's melody was better than ours and then chose to believe our song needed to be tucked in the corner of our souls while we then spent our own God given time and energy helping another person create theirs. The more we played the strings of another person's tune, the less we were able to hear our own until one day we realized we felt empty and unfulfilled.

Throughout our journey we forgot to remind ourselves of this truth. In our own power of choice and free will, we made a conscious effort to tune out our song and only create another's. This is a truly empowering epiphany because knowing we had a choice to make, we now understand the same power of choice to make another decision as well. Even though we convinced ourselves of the illusion that another person's passion and purpose was more important than ours, we can choose to make another decision and place our purpose as a priority.

We often realize we are unfulfilled when we are sitting at a place of employment that we are miserable at, or in a relationship with another person who no longer serves our greater purpose. It isn't until our heart has yearned to feel love and joy when we come to the crossroads of having to make a decision. Although making the obvious choice of choosing love over fear appears simple enough, it is often the action that becomes the challenge. Since we are creatures of habit we create patterns of love or fear that bring in experiences to support our most dominant emotion.

Choosing to be happy is the first step, and realizing we have our own song that needs to be heard is the passion that will lead us to play our song. If your song is created from being a wonderful mother or teacher, then your soul will play the melody and your role is to hear that melody and own the creation of it. If your melody is about starting your own company and being your own boss, then your role is to create the song from the Source within you. Whatever melody is playing in your soul, you must create that song through thoughts, emotions and actions that support bringing your song to life.

Realize your role in this journey through life is to create your own life in the loving and joyous manner you were meant to experience it. Through prayer and purpose you will learn to create miracles in your life that you once thought were impossible. Reach beyond your own self-imposed limitations and realize the only limits are those you have placed within your own illusions. Use the power of prayer, the power of love, and the power of God to create the life of your dreams. Play your song and the world will sing with you Miracle Workers!

What is my soul song that has been resonating in my heart?

_____

_____

_____

_____

_____

_____

_____

Rather than attempt to quiet my song, what can I do to create it in my life?

_____

_____

_____

_____

_____

_____

_____

What is God whispering into my soul about my song and ways to express my melody?

_____

_____

_____

_____

_____

_____

_____

_____

_____

_____

_____

_____

_____

_____

_____

_____

_____

"When thought, love, and action are combined to create a dreamers' world, then people look from the outside in and say it was only because they were lucky or wealthy to begin with. Truth is the only remedy for lost souls. When those souls recognize the truth they are running away from is the truth of their own souls, they too will realize the creation of all they desire lies within them alone. Lucky, miracle, special... all of these words represent each and every soul walking the earth."

Excerpt from Through the Eyes of Truth –
A Conversation with God about My Life, Your Life, and Discovering Our Purpose

Creating Utopia
Living as a Miracle Worker Day 20

I AM A LUCKY CHILD

How many times have you acknowledged this truth in your life? Seriously, how often are you in gratitude for being a lucky child of God? When I began seeing myself as lucky, I began noticing my experiences supported my perception of self. I met and married my soul mate, competition goals, became a published author, and a personal and spiritual development coach. Every day I am in gratitude to God for blessing me and making me a lucky child. People will even ask me if I realize how lucky I am, and my answer is always "yes I do... and so are you."

However often their puzzled expression reflects the doubt in their mind. They usually follow the expression with several heartfelt reasons why they are *not* a lucky child and completely contradict me. What they failed to hear was that they in fact are a lucky child but they believe an illusion that says otherwise. One of the most difficult patterns to break are those that create the support of love. We so often believe that we are our conditions and in order for us to receive love from self and love from God, then those conditions must no longer exist.

If we change our perspective to realize the truth which is that we are not our conditions and they no more define us than another person's opinion of us does. We must remain fixated on truth and the only way to see truth is to follow the eyes of God as we walk the path of creation with Source. It becomes harder to create our greatest goals when we have our eyes off of love and on the world of fear and conditions. Realize as a child of the great *I AM*, abundance of everything that brings you love is your birthright! I don't believe God places conditions on us, but through fear we place conditions upon ourselves which in turn separates us from our Creator.

Realize this moment that you are blessed and live your days in those moments of grace when you feel blessed. Tell yourself you are a child of the Creator and are very much a lucky child. You are as lucky as the individual who wins a million-dollar contest drawing, you are as lucky as the person who creates their dream home out of thin air, and you are as lucky as your perfect and beautiful soul allows yourself to be. God cannot gift us with His grace if we refuse to accept that gift. We must be in gratitude of receiving all the love Source is blessing us with daily. The best ways to receive love is to be open and in gratitude daily.

This means although you are having a bad day at work, be grateful for your health or the fact you are now connecting to your passion and purpose. You have only one life on this precious journey and your gift to self is to accept the greatest forms of love through the hands of God and see yourself through the eyes of truth. You are Miracle Workers and have every right to expect your greatest dreams to manifest before your eyes. Your role as a co-creator is to be an active participant with God in the creation of your greatest vision of your life!

What are some areas in my life where I consider myself lucky?

_____

_____

_____

_____

_____

_____

_____

_____

How do I define luck and how can I always perceive myself as being a lucky child?

_____

_____

_____

_____

_____

_____

_____

_____

What is God whispering into my soul about being a lucky child?

_____

_____

_____

_____

_____

_____

_____

_____

_____

_____

_____

_____

_____

_____

_____

_____

"Seek not the advice nor the approval from the world around you. Close your ears to those who shout illusion from the walls of their fear. They seek not to hinder you but to claim that which is not theirs. You have only to hear my voice and seek my truth in order to find your greatest blessings lying waiting for you among green pastures. If you falter in your faith and choose not to answer the call before manifesting your vision, then how can that dream you desire to create be seen? For I call forth not those who are standing boasting through their pride. Instead I call the meek who seek to know truth before deceit, and honor me before they honor themselves."

Excerpt from Creating Utopia
Living Life as a Miracle Worker

Creating Utopia
Living as a Miracle Worker Day 21

BEING IN ALIGNMENT

When we truly understand that our dream lies within us instead of outside of us, we are able to align ourselves with the connection to that dream. Now instead of expending our energy on seeking approval from another person for our perfect goal, we need to seek the connection of that goal within. Being in alignment is about being connected to the fact your dream already exists. Your thoughts must be as one with already having that goal in your life. Then your emotions will support being in gratitude of the presence of your goal so finally your actions will continually be working on a physical level of that goal in your life.

For instance, if you desire to empower people from all around the world by being a role model, spokesperson, or advocate then ask yourself how are you going to accomplish this? As you allow your mind to wrap around engaging people and providing them tools to develop a deeper relationship with themselves, then do your actions and your emotions reflect excitement and inspiration? Who are you contacting in order to reach a broader audience? Is there a niche you are reaching or a universal message? Are you empowering women by aligning with them or building a dream home within your soul one step at a time? Do you feel empowered when you write out your speech, or encourage people through entries in your blog? How are you connecting to the people you desire to reach? How does it feel on a soul level to be living your purpose?

In this example you dig a little deeper and align yourself with your dream now at a deeper level. As your thoughts wrap around standing in front of an audience, you envision yourself already having this goal in your present moment. Now you begin searching your thoughts as you define what your life appears like with the completion of this goal. What are you doing with your time throughout the days after your workshops? What does your first week look like, your first month or your life quarter by quarter? If you are advocating for a cause or wanting to create a ripple effect of positive energy, then how are you doing that? Look at your goal and define what that means to you. There is no right or wrong answer, just the specific definition of how you align yourself with your goal on a mind, body, and soul connection.

As your emotions fill with joy in the thoughts of having this experience, then what actions are you taking to support the continuation of this love and joy in your heart? If you want to inspire the world with your story, then are you already blogging on topics that will create a ripple effect of positive energy? If your goal is to empower other women then how are you doing that today? By realizing that being in alignment of your dream means that you alone have the power to live within its present at this very moment, then choose to own your greatest goals and live your life as if they are already in existence.

Keep celebrating your life and honoring your gifts. Through prayer and being a co-creator in your life with God, you can make any dream a reality. Seize your moments of creation and live the life of your dreams today. Remember that as a child of God, abundance in everything that brings you love and joy is your birthright, so own your life Miracle Worker!

How do I create alignment with my goals in my life?

_____

_____

_____

_____

_____

_____

_____

What can I do daily to always remain in alignment of my God and my dreams?

_____

_____

_____

_____

_____

_____

_____

_____

What is God whispering into my soul about being aligned with my greatest dreams?

_____

_____

_____

_____

_____

_____

_____

_____

_____

_____

_____

_____

_____

_____

_____

_____

"Utopia is a state of mind my child, much like being in a state of peace and love and this begins and ends within the soul. Ask yourself if there was one dream you could create today, what would that dream be like? For I have instilled within each of you a blueprint so authentic that only you have the power and the passion to create it from the inside out. What would you create today if you knew your miracle needed only to survive on your thoughts, emotions, and actions? I tell you this my child, your soul can no longer deceive itself by looking at the world outside and calling it truth. You know what your creative energy has made, and soon the world will discover theirs as well by seeking guidance from within."

Excerpt from Creating Utopia –
Living Life as a Miracle Worker

Creating Utopia
Living as a Miracle Worker Day 22

YOU ARE UTOPIA

I believe we are all energy beings having a physical experience and not the other way around. How else can we explain the presence of God and us being one with Source energy? If we remind ourselves that we are more than our body and more than our experiences, we can remain connected in the truth of our own existence. As energy beings we then remember that we do not need to be in the physical to be as one with our greatest dreams. Utopia represents a state of being not a physical activity. Knowing this we can relish in the being as one with our dreams at any given moment in our lives. Then we can use the power we have been given as co-creators in our own lives to truly create those experiences that reflect our greatest vision of ourselves.

Every day we have the choice to create our lives through the experiences of love or fear. Although we cannot control anything in the world outside of us, we can control how we act, think, and feel. We get to choose to create a state of bliss in any situation just by how we use our own creative abilities. Utopia is not separate from us as it lies within us. It is no more separate from us than our greatest dreams are. If you desire to experience the thrill of winning any competition, you need to first connect to that state of bliss within you. This reminds you that you are as connected to your dream as you are to utopia.

Continuing to be in alignment and connected to your greatest dream throughout the moments of your life when you are experiencing emotions of fear will help you realize the manifestation of that dream sooner. Ask yourself how you can find ways of connecting to the emotions of already having your goal before seeing the evidence of it will help you to think proactively. What can you do throughout your day to remain connected to your joy even though the illusion that surrounds you may be contradictory? If you are working at a job that does not fulfill you then focus your energy on the parts of the job you do enjoy. If you are competing in a fitness competition, allow yourself to create the emotions of joy the definition of the win will create in your life.

Allowing yourself permission to remain focused on your reality rather than your illusion will keep you connected to God and to your own truth. There is nothing outside of you that will bring you more connected to your joy than what lies within you. Utopia is a state of bliss and as you remain connected to God then you grow your love of self, love of Source, and love of your dream. This is the only time you have so remain connected to being present and in the moment of your life. This is where you create your future, so continue living a life of joy and be the Miracle Workers you were created to be!

How do I create Utopia in my life?

_____

_____

_____

_____

_____

_____

_____

How can I remain connected and perceive myself as one with my greatest dream?

_____

_____

_____

_____

_____

_____

_____

What is God whispering into my soul about being aligned with my greatest dreams?

_____

_____

_____

_____

_____

_____

_____

_____

_____

_____

_____

_____

_____

_____

_____

_____

"So when you turn on the news and discover that another lucky soul has won wealth beyond their expectations, understand the person who is experiencing winning the lottery is the person who already understood on a soul level they were going to win. This is just as powerful as the boy who is staying up late studying his math to become a teacher, or the young teenage girl who is practicing her lab study to get into medical school. The same can be said for the talented athlete who was born into a family with very little money yet possesses great love for their talent, and will someday light up the court with a professional team endorsement. These souls all won the "lottery" in their own right. For their purpose was to experience what their soul truly loved, and in the process became very successful and abundant."

Excerpt from Through the Eyes of Truth –
A Conversation with God about My Life, Your Life, and Discovering Our Purpose

Creating Utopia
Living as a Miracle Worker Day 23

SETTING GREAT EXPECTATIONS

Living as a Miracle Worker does not mean that we need to seek perfection outside of us, rather seek the connection to God and our greatest potential within us. One of the problems we encounter when doing this is that we have been taught from an early age to conform to the expectations placed upon us from the world outside of us. As children we learn to adapt to meet our parent's expectations so we can be rewarded. Then we rise to meet expectations placed upon us during childhood at school or when learning to play sports. This makes it easier to transition into adulthood where we meet expectations placed upon us from our employers, society, and our life partners.

Very rarely do we take the time to ask ourselves what expectations we desire to meet when it comes to creating our own life. Often this is because we spend so much time trying to meet the standard the world outside places upon us that we forget we can create a new level of expectations within us. Why would you ask, would we want to create new demands upon ourselves when we are struggling to meet those set outside of us? Because we are here in this experience of life to first serve ourselves and our greater purpose. Then the world's expectations should come in second…. not the other way around. But rarely do we stop in the moments of our day and take note that often we are reacting to the world's expectations rather than meeting our own. Why does this matter?

Look at the world around you and ask yourself how many people do you see daily who are living their lives as Miracle Workers? Again, I don't mean in the perfect sense of the word. I am referring to those souls who wake up every morning in gratitude for their lives and creating their own blueprint in the world. Those souls who reach beyond their own self-imposed limitations and work daily to create their lives through their God given gifts. Those same gifts which make them feel joyous and connected to a greater purpose. Now ask yourself how you would recognize these souls. First they tend to perceive life through the eyes of truth. They realize their circumstances do not define them. They spend minimal time complaining and gossiping about others and more time being in gratitude and working on creating the life of their dreams.

Now ask yourself again how many people you know on a personal level who spend their time being in gratitude and living as Miracle Workers? By learning to set your own life expectations, you connect with God and with your greater potential. You no longer need to live for the world outside of yourself but learn to balance being a co-creator with God in your own life while enjoying the gifts of co-creation with the world outside of you. Remind yourself daily that you are experiencing this illusion filled world in order to create the life of your dreams. You are the miracle in this journey through life so celebrate it and live a life of joy Miracle Workers!

What daily expectations am I living my life trying to meet?

_____

_____

_____

_____

_____

_____

_____

What personal expectations do I desire in my life in order to live a life of purpose and passion?

_____

_____

_____

_____

_____

_____

_____

What is God whispering into my soul about being a Miracle Worker in my own life?

_____

_____

_____

_____

_____

_____

_____

_____

_____

_____

_____

_____

_____

_____

_____

_____

"When you awaken to the truth that failure is as much an illusion as is fear, then you will understand the greatness of who you are. Yet rather than dismiss the emotions and thoughts of failure, so many souls choose to identify with those emotions of fear and disappointment, thus they cannot separate themselves from the feelings. This in turn creates the unity of the emotions of disappointment. The feelings become so overwhelming that it consumes the soul until they cannot separate their own soul from their feelings."

Excerpt from Through the Eyes of Truth –
A Conversation with God about My Life, Your Life, and Discovering Our Purpose

Creating Utopia
Living as a Miracle Worker Day 24

PUSHING BEYOND THE DISAPPOINTMENT

Let's face it, our illusion is often filled with disappointments. It feels as if we cannot change the outcome of our circumstances, so we then attempt to adjust our dreams. We convince ourselves that we cannot have the dreams our hearts are calling us to create, so we instead choose to convince ourselves of an illusion that we are not Miracle Workers. As a result, we often tuck our greatest dreams into the corner of our mind and pretend they do not exist. We then spend our moments, days and years creating a life that doesn't fill our greatest potential. We do this without realizing the more we create our life from fear, the more emotions of fear we create.

Remember as co-creators in our life we create our experiences through love or fear. If we are in a continual state of fear then through our thoughts, emotions, and actions, we create more fear. Even if we are not aware of how we are creating our lives, we still create nonetheless. What we need to do is become very aware of what emotions we are using to glorify our journey through this life. We need to be aware of our motivation when entering any contest or perceived competition where one prize is the reward. Here is why...

As you have already discovered, the journey through any perceived competition is an illusion. Since you have the power to create your greatest dreams then we have the power to create the emotions and thoughts that already support having that dream in your life today. Then your actions will follow and help you manifest it through the law of life and the law of attraction. When you dismiss your greatest goals, we create an immediate emotion of disappointment which is derived from fear. If spending enough time creating disappointment in your own life by denying yourself your dreams, you risk this emotion becoming your new normal. You do not even realize that by denying yourself the right to create love in your own life through the power of your gifts, you deny yourself self-love and self-acceptance.

Becoming a deliberate co-creator in your life with God will help you realize your greatest dreams moment by moment. Rather than succumbing to the old patterns of thoughts that created disappointment, you work hand in hand with Source to create new experiences and new love into your life. Then will your new patterns be comfortable because you have pushed yourself beyond self-imposed limitations of fear. This is your life and through free will you get to choose how you will live it. Relish every moment and reach within to make your greatest dreams a reality! Live life to the fullest and you will continue to celebrate being Miracle Workers!

What disappointing feelings have I been creating in my daily life?

_____

_____

_____

_____

_____

_____

_____

What dreams have I tucked away because I am in fear of being disappointed?

_____

_____

_____

_____

_____

_____

_____

_____

What is God whispering into my soul about breaking the patterns of disappointment and fear?

"Each of you have the ability to create such beauty and joy in your own lives, and if you would only seek truth of self from within then you would discover yourself the way I see you. If you could only see your glory through the illusion you have chosen to create, you would never spend another day wasting time and energy painting in the same box you were taught to paint your life in as a child. You would magnify the glory I have given you by celebrating your soul which is where you will discover your purpose. You were never created to become an imitation of one another. Instead, you are all called to discover your own unique gifts and use those gifts to bring more love and joy into your own lives. Only then will you cease from seeking your glory in a world outside of you."

**Excerpt from Creating Utopia –
Living Life as a Miracle Worker**

Creating Utopia
Living as a Miracle Worker Day 25

RIGHTEOUS INDIGNATION: WHAT ARE YOU FIGHTING FOR?

One of the blessings of listening to God is that we are led into truth to discover our passion and honor our purpose. However, we may resist because we do not fully understand the bigger picture or the cause we are connecting inspiration for. What happens when we resist our greatest calling is that our soul bears the burden of experiencing conflict. We feel torn between the possibilities of what can be with the familiarity of what currently is. How then do we transition from the comfort of fear and sameness to the shift of inspiration and empowerment?

I believe that so often our greatest opponent in the creation of our dreams is ourselves. We desire to create a new experience of love and joy, yet our souls resist the change because we fear either being unworthy of receiving this lofty goal or we fear the unknown and how our lives will change once we receive it. We become obstinate and indignant, blaming others or even God because we refuse to accept responsibility for changing something in our lives that will allow us to connect with our dreams. I refer to this as righteous indignation. We look around at the world around us and argue with God as to why we should change when we perceive others as having more success and they do not appear any worthier than we do.

The problem is that our perception creates our greatest dreams, not the perception of the world around us. Although any competition may appear to be for the lucky or favored few, the fact remains you create your own luck through your perception of how you value yourself. Too often when you ask Source for something new in your life, you need to change an old perception which is often tied to a pattern of behavior. You are then asked to change a behavior and instead of agreeing to do this, you become indignant and find reasons why you should not have to change in order to receive something new that creates love in your life.

What God is ultimately asking you to do is replace fear with love, and the way we continue creating fear in our lives is through our thoughts, emotions, and actions. Instead of being co-creators with God on the same goal, we find reasons to argue. We look at the world around us and convince ourselves the latest celebrity, role model, or titleholder is no better than us because ... (fill in the blank) Instead of creating a new way of thinking, we become resentful and judge those around us for not being good enough when in fact, it is ourselves we fail to find worthy.

Then our resentment grows as does our judgement towards those who have the experiences we desire to create. Since we are all connected then our judgement comes back to us tenfold and the patterns continue repeating themselves until we change or we don't. So ask yourself today what you are being righteously indignant about. What do you refuse to change so you can have a new experience of love? When you learn to be honest with yourself and ask God to reveal truth to you, realize you cannot go back to deceiving yourself.

You are a magnificent co-creator and your greatest dreams are just waiting to be realized. How will you change your illusion in order to create abundance of joy, passion, and love in your life? Realize that God asks us to change our perspective in order to change our experiences, so rather than pretending we are not in control, let's empower ourselves to realize we are Miracle Workers and through the power of God, all things are possible!

What specific patterns of fear are you being called upon to change in your life?

_____

_____

_____

_____

_____

_____

_____

What are you being righteously indignant about changing and why?

_____

_____

_____

_____

_____

_____

_____

_____

What is God whispering into my soul about my righteous indignations?

"Money is nothing more than an exchange of energy, and is nothing without the value that is placed upon it. A soul may never feel as if they have enough money until they realize that money is not what their soul seeks. The soul seeks expression of self to create love. Only when you realize this, will you understand what it means to be rich."

Excerpt from Through the Eyes of Truth –
A Conversation with God about My Life, Your Life, and Discovering Our Purpose

Creating Utopia
Living as a Miracle Worker Day 26

IT'S NOT ABOUT THE MONEY

Money is one of those tangible excuses we use to create more love or fear in our lives. We find reasons for not achieving our greatest dreams due to the lack of it, or discover new ways to find ourselves unworthy of receiving more because others do not have what we have. In other words, so many of us tend to use money as a weapon against ourselves to grow into our greatness or separate ourselves from our greatest dreams. Why? At what point in our lives did we believe an illusion that as energy, our life experiences depend on one particular source?

Think about it. Most of us can open our wallets and find some money in there, and to some it may be enough and to others it isn't enough at all. However, the point is that we all have some amount of money. When do we ask ourselves at what point we place limits on the amount of currency we are worth? If money is just tangible energy and we all have some of it, then why do we use the lack of it to create more lack? Could we assume that as energy beings having a physical experience, we create our world through our thoughts, emotions, and actions? If so, then do we support our fears of unworthiness through creating limits that reinforce our emotions and thoughts about not feeling worthy?

In other words, what if we are creating the lack of money to support our perspective of fear rather than being in fear because we have minimal amount of money? How would you convince yourself that you can create the money you already have in your bank account yet are limited to creating any more without the permission of another person to give it to you through increased salary or a monetary gift? So often we use the excuse of money to support creating fear and then place ourselves in competitive situations that support our belief of not being worthy to create more money.

Money allows us to experience certain things, but we all have the power to create so much love and joy in our lives. Instead of being in a position of gratitude for what we have, often we continue our restlessness and emotions of fear because we still yearn for something more. More money, a bigger home, or a new car, that will provide you the recognition you seek from yourself. What if you were competing to get your own approval instead of the approval from another person? How would that change the way you perceive a competition or a grand prize?

If you look at the world around us, you relate most to those experiences and people who connect to what you love or fear. Looking at money in the same manner allows you to notice your relationship to yourself and to the limits you have placed in your own life. I don't believe that our self-imposed limitations come down to the amount of money we have, but to our *relationship* with the money we have. If you fear your own greatness you may find yourself remaining stuck in your limiting thoughts of lack. However, if you accept your own connection to God and to your birthright of abundance, you may be able to shift your perspective and realize your greatness lies not in your wealth but in your love.

Enjoy your lives Miracle Workers and continue reaching beyond your self-imposed limitations. Honor your God whisper and realize that utopia is not a place but a state of being. You have the power at any point in your life to connect to the divine within you and create an abundance of love and joy so seize your moments of creation!

What is your relationship with money in your own life?

_____

_____

_____

_____

_____

_____

_____

What dreams have you ignored due to the perceived lack of money?

_____

_____

_____

_____

_____

_____

_____

What is God whispering into my soul about my relationship with money?

_____

_____

_____

_____

_____

_____

_____

_____

_____

_____

_____

_____

_____

_____

_____

_____

_____

_____

"If your purpose through this point in your life was to know God on a deeper level then you must know the truth of all there is. Nothing separates you and I except for your perception of separateness. Nothing separates you from a loved one who has crossed over except for your perception of separateness. If you and I are one and I am one with all that is, then you and all that is must be one as well. Yet this truth creates such a fear in your life, it almost becomes too difficult to bear when you have to think about death. My child death is not the end of life, but the expression of the soul from transitioning from one awareness into the next. It is not to be feared unless you fear God."

**Excerpt from Creating Utopia –
Living Life as a Miracle Worker**

Creating Utopia
Living as a Miracle Worker Day 27

ACCEPTING YOUR PURPOSE

We live in a world where we have been convinced our reality lies in what we see and our illusion lies within in what we feel. Somehow many of us have not yet found the balance of understanding how to walk in an illusion filled world while maintaining being grounded in our own reality. How do we do this and still be able to discern truth from illusion? Through your connection to God and your connection to self. Realizing we are spirit beings having a physical experience allows us to balance our heart and our logic. While many of us focus only on the physical world and what we see with our physical eyes, we often forget that we are creating our physical experiences through what we cannot see…. our energy and focused attention.

The times in our lives this creates a problem is when we live only by our sight and forget we are creating the unseen. Our purpose lies not in the world outside of us through others telling us what we should do to life a magical life. Our purpose is discovered within us when we are connecting to our passion. As we all know, our passion is an intangible, an energy that allows us to create the emotions of love and joy. When we are able to look within ourselves to discover those passions, we are then able to turn them into a tangible experience in the physical world outside of us. I believe however the problem arises when we seek to uncover our purpose and only rely on the world outside of us to tell us what that is.

We can ask those around us to provide us hints of what they feel our purpose is, but your purpose is connected to God, so why not get it straight from the Source? In other words, you need to seek your purpose within yourself so you can experience it outside of you. When we get aligned with our purpose we are more accepting of creating it in our life without the need for approval from another person. After all, why would you seek approval from another person who is not living their purpose? We would expect their answer to be shared by the philosophy that they live their lives by. If they have succumbed to pressure from the world outside of them to do what others think they should do, whether it brings them joy or not, they will more than likely advise you to do the same.

In order to connect with your purpose, you need to seek truth from Source through prayer and by realizing you need to act on those ideas you are receiving through your God whispers. These ideas may be new to you or even dare you to move beyond your own self-imposed limiting thoughts, but they will ultimately lead you to doing what creates more love and joy in your life. Often when we pray, we ask God to reveal to us our purpose. When Source answers through God whispers, you are often asked to take certain actions that support the evidence of your goal already in your life, and gather momentum towards your purpose and passion.

In God's eyes the miracle or dream has already been created, so you are being led to the connection of that dream by doing those things today that you would ultimately do when you would see them evident in the world outside of you. If you ask God to reveal your purpose and Source tells you to write a book and share it with the world, you must honor your God whisper even though there is no evidence the world desires to read your book. Trusting your intuition or your God whispers will develop your connected to Source and your connection to self on a level you were not even aware you are capable of! Seek truth from within and realize your purpose lies within you and bringing the experience to life through thought, emotions, and actions will lead you to a life of your dreams.

Continue living in truth and trust your connection to God through the power of prayer. Your life was intended to be enjoyed by you and the best way to know what will bring you joy is to step outside of the comfort level you are in now. The same comfort that is bringing you the similar patterns of creating fear and lack of fulfillment in your life. Always remember that you are a child of God and abundance of every dream you have the power to create within is your birthright. Enjoy your life Miracle Workers and you will continue creating more miracles!

What is your purpose in this life?

_____

_____

_____

_____

_____

_____

_____

How can you create passion and purpose in your life on a daily basis?

_____

_____

_____

_____

_____

_____

_____

What is God whispering into my soul about finding my purpose?

_____

_____

_____

_____

_____

_____

_____

_____

_____

_____

_____

_____

_____

_____

_____

_____

"Awaken to the possibility of that which you wish to experience is already present and seeking you as well. As the creator and the observer you are in fact creating the experience for yourself. Every soul is born into the physical realm with the same creative capabilities, so you need not justify your desires of self-expression to another. Nor do you owe your energy to another who has chosen not to follow their own passions. Your role is to enjoy your moments of co-creation and seize the enjoyment of life as you know it."

Excerpt from Creating Utopia–
Living Life as a Miracle Worker

Creating Utopia
Living as a Miracle Worker Day 28

YOU ARE THE OBSERVER AND THE CREATOR

As a co-creator in your life you need to remember that you are a perfect spiritual being having an imperfect physical experience. As one with God you are to align yourself to your goals and connect with them on a mind, body, and soul level. Whether you are on a quest for self-discovery or on a personal challenge to create your new dream home, realize that you are both the observer and the creator in this experience.

As you are experiencing disappointments throughout your journey into any competition or challenge to achieve a goal, I think you often lose sight of being the creator. Look at the world in which you live as a perfect example. So much of your time is spent in front of computers or your phones as you are observing the world. You often watch the television first thing in the morning and expose yourself to the news which oftentimes is inundated with fear. Then you observe your computers and those around you at school or work, only to come home and watch the world around you through television again or the social media.

Now let's shift your perspective and realize you can create more than you observe through your relationship with yourselves. As you are watching people around you, often you shift into the observer's frame of reference. This often creates patterns of comfort as you become content watching the world around you rather than being actively involved in it. Then you try to shift your attention within when you attempt to play the role of the creator which can make you uncomfortable. Then you entertain possibilities of dreams and lofty goals, but not completely certain of your own creative ability to achieve them.

As you follow through on a few attempts to create your dreams, you allow your heart to become excited about the possibility of having that dream become a reality. When you do not connect to it, you then convince yourself that you are unlucky or unworthy of having this goal. However, what you often fail to understand is that you *first* thought of yourself as unlucky or unworthy and your actions followed your own relationship with self and with your deepest dreams.

Your thoughts create your emotions which in turn create your actions. You may dream of buying a new house, yet continually remind yourself why you are not worthy of having it. Maybe you desire to experience a loving relationship, but feel unloved by self. Since you attract the energy you put out, then you may attract another person who also fails to love themselves as well. You cannot expect the world to give you something you have failed to create, because you are in fact the creator of love in your own life. This includes the people and experiences that bring you abundant joy and love.

When you balance your role of observer and creator, you are able to watch the world outside of you and become inspired by people who connect with your energy. Maybe you witness a stranger receive a reward or win a prize and you become excited for that person because you know you too have the power within you to create your own miracles. Then you can transition into the role of creator and observer and realize you are a perfect spiritual being having a creative physical experience. Live your life as a Miracle Worker and build the foundation of your greatest dreams from the passion in your heart!

What have you observed about your greatest dream for your life?

_____

_____

_____

_____

_____

_____

_____

_____

What can you do to create this dream into your life?

_____

_____

_____

_____

_____

_____

_____

_____

What is God whispering into my soul about creating my dream?

_____

_____

_____

_____

_____

_____

_____

_____

_____

_____

_____

_____

_____

_____

_____

_____

"So much of the problem arises when you witness the manifestation of another soul's dream and see it in its entirety. This dream may appear to you as an expensive car, an extravagant lifestyle, or the abundance of wealth. Because you see the appearance of this dream in its fullest form, you fail to realize this dream was created through tiny moments of thought and energy. What you see is the outcome of the dream and not the process that soul took to create this beautiful manifestation through years of hard work and disciplined thoughts. Because you see only the result and fail to understand the creative process, you are quick to label it as luck or destiny, when in fact this soul or groups of souls created their own destiny."

**Excerpt from Creating Utopia—
Living Life as a Miracle Worker**

Creating Utopia
Living as a Miracle Worker Day 29

HOPE VS. FAITH

Our dreams are a part of our soul as much as God is and I believe when we stifle our creative process to experience our greatest dreams, we limit Source and what we are capable of. So much of our experiences come down to the hope to have more joy and love in our lives and the faith to walk the journey into the unknown. If you attempt to create a dream out of just hope, you risk withering under the fear of stepping outside of your comfort zone in order to achieve it. After all, a dream represents an experience that is currently not present in your life, so you need to shift your energy in some form to connect to the unseen.

I believe in order to achieve any new goal, you need to balance hope and faith in your journey. Your hope of experiencing the next level of joy through creation needs to be followed by the faith to take action and move towards that goal. The beginning of creating the goal is the seed planted, and with every step towards bringing that goal to life is your way of loving and nourishing that dream. You seek the evidence of the goal everyday like you are looking for the evidence of life through the tiny seed that you water, and then it finally sprouts and reveals the truth of its own beauty. Your role is to walk in the faith that every step you take towards the sprouting of your dream will eventually be revealed to you in the right time.

If you only have hope, then you will not take the proper action towards creating the dream. Remember that you create through thought, emotion, and action, so not working on all three elements of creating may only lead to hoping that your dream will somehow manifest itself out of thin air. This isn't creation... it's imagination. Although you may try to convince yourself of this, you cannot lie to your own soul. Because you attempt to convince yourself of an illusion then you create fear and more experiences of fear to support your illusion. You may think that you need to manipulate or deceive others into giving you what you think you are in search of, all the while forgetting that your soul seeks expression through creation. You never need to earn the worthiness of receiving a prize when the gift is in the journey of creating your dream. Rather than setting limits on your dreams, ask God to reveal your truth and walk hand in hand in the creation of your greatest vision of yourself. Your creative abilities go beyond just hoping your goals will happen.

Your power of free will allows you to create your life with Source and be an active participant in the journey. If you do not feel connected to the outcome of your personal goal or any dream you wish to experience, then you may not have yet aligned with that dream. Every step you take through your journey in life is about learning to tap into your greatest goals and create those experiences that bring you love and joy. This goes beyond hope, but hope is the first step to creating the life of your dreams. Grant yourself permission to discover yourself as a co-creator in your own life and you will realize the difference between won and own is only a matter of perception. Keep living your life as Miracle Workers and believe in the power of your dreams!

What dream am I hoping will happen in my life?

_____

_____

_____

_____

_____

_____

_____

How am I walking in faith towards my goal?

_____

_____

_____

_____

_____

_____

_____

What is God whispering into my soul about walking in faith?

_____

_____

_____

_____

_____

_____

_____

_____

_____

_____

_____

_____

_____

_____

_____

_____

"Be still and know that by sharing your gift and your story, some will relate to the experience of knowing their soul and learning to trust in their power of prayer. Through these pages and through the love from these words, the truth will be the message. You are called to deliver that truth to another who will learn from it, and seek their own through prayer."

Excerpt from Through the Eyes of Truth –
A Conversation with God about My Life, Your Life, and Discovering Our Purpose.

Creating Utopia
Living as a Miracle Worker Day 30

WRITE YOUR STORY

Your instrument of creating is your physical body, as it transposes the song in your heart to a symphony through the power of your own hands. Whether your melody creates a dance across a marathon or a new life goal, you are the conductor and can express it in the manner which brings you the greatest joy. If you desire to sing with the loudest voice then stand on your own personal stage and share your song with yourself first, and those who are like energy to you will be inspired to find their own voice as well.

If you desire to dance across the streets to the tune of your own melody, then dance in such a manner that your feet will bring you a greater level of self-love. Whatever your song is, sing it to the heavens because this is your only life here on this specific journey. You are not meant to be imitations of those people around you, but instead are co-creators in your life to be the most amazing and authentic version of yourself ever created! Rather than trying to dance to another person's music, write your own song. Let your life be the perfect story of your own soul, so when the day comes that you cross through the veil of illusion into the hands of God you will smile with wonder and amazement. You are a child of God and are created to magnify your soul through your own talents and gifts.

Find your passion and live your purpose, so you never have to wonder what you were capable of. What if you looked in the mirror today, and instead of seeing the tiny wrinkles forming around your beautiful face you decided to make a magnificent dream come true? Realizing there is no such thing as too tall, too thin, too old, or too young, you created your own dreams by writing your story word by word. Wouldn't it be more magnificent to you to uncover your own hidden gifts and turn those into dreams that will someday inspire another person? These gifts do not have to inspire the entire world, but allow them first to create love in your life. Only then will you be able to bring love into another's life through letting them understand there are millions of tiny formulas to create dreams that have yet to be shared.

Stop trying to do what another does, and be what another person is and learn to embrace your own greatness. Every day that passes with you looking past yourself as if you are invisible is another day you become invisible to yourself. Look into the mirror and instead of noticing the tiny imperfections, see the eyes of truth staring back at you... the eyes of God. If you are one with the Creator, then begin looking for the reflection of God back at you and someday you will realize the power you have to make the greatest dreams come true. Inspire another by inspiring yourself first and you will create a ripple effect of inspiration and hope.

Honor your journey in this life because it is such a fragile and beautiful gift. Treat yourself like the child of God you are and bless yourself with the fruits of your own hands. These past 30 days is a way for you to create new patterns in your life that serve your greater good. Whether you want to build your dream home brick by brick, or create a new home of love and peace within your own soul, realize that you already own the dream you desire to see manifested. All you have to do is ask God to guide you through a journey of self-discovery where you will reach within to your own wonder and tap into the power of God. The rest is magic…. be your own magic Miracle Workers and continue to live inspired!

What story am I hoping to write in my own life?

_____

_____

_____

_____

_____

_____

_____

How can I actively write my story word for word through my thoughts, emotions and actions?

_____

_____

_____

_____

_____

_____

_____

What is God whispering into my soul about my life story?

_____

_____

_____

_____

_____

_____

_____

_____

_____

_____

_____

_____

_____

_____

_____

_____

_____

Other Books by Suzy Bootz

Creating Utopia – Living Life as a Miracle Worker – Available on Amazon

Through the Eyes of Truth – A Conversation with God about My Life, Your Life, and Discovering Our Purpose – Available on Audio on Audible.com and Print on Amazon

Through the Eyes of Truth Workbook – Available on Amazon

God Whispers - Daily Devotional for Inspired Living – Available on Amazon

Heaven Scent – Love Letters from Beyond: Available on Amazon

Follow Us!

- Instagram: @realsuzybootz
- Twitter: @realsuzybootz
- Facebook: suzybootz
- Blog: www.suzybootz.com

To live inspired please visit www.suzybootz.com

www.ingramcontent.com/pod-product-compliance
Lightning Source LLC
Chambersburg PA
CBHW081510040426
42447CB00013B/3182